The
Quaker Tapestry
Guide
in Colour

Quaker Tapestry Scheme 1992

The Quaker Tapestry Guide first published in 1989
Supplement published 1990
Exhibition Guide published 1991

The Quaker Tapestry Guide in Colour replaces the above mentioned publications. The Committee of the Quaker Tapestry Scheme wishes to record its profound gratitude to those individuals, Quaker meetings and trusts who have contributed to the cost of publication. The text of *The Quaker Tapestry Guide* has been revised under the direction of the committee which reiterates its gratitude to those who prepared the original designs and text.

Printed by Lithographics Ltd, Worcester, England.
Unit 1A, Everoak Estate, Bromyard Road, Worcester WR2 5HN.

Contents

The order of the panels in this book requires some explanation. It is based on the chapters of *Christian faith and practice* which, with *Church government*, forms the *Book of Christian discipline* of the Yearly Meeting of Friends in Britain, officially known as London Yearly Meeting. This discipline "is not something imposed from without, a discipline of law, but...is a quality of the spirit" and is a discipline "we lay upon ourselves and corporately accept" as the Yearly Meeting minuted in 1967. Our Yearly Meeting has therefore been accustomed to revise the *Book of discipline* approximately once in each generation. The text of *Christian faith and practice* was approved in 1959 and that of *Church government* in 1967. Both are at present being revised and the ordering of the panels may not reflect that of the next revision. The titles of each section are, however, those of chapters in the present *Christian faith and practice*.

Acknowledgements

The Committee of the Quaker Tapestry Scheme is indebted to many Friends for their help in the design of the panels illustrated in the following pages, and for the compilation of the text. In addition to Anne Wynn-Wilson who has designed many panels herself and has supervised all the designs, the following are the major contributors, although help was given by many others:

Joe McCrum, Margery Levy, David Butler, Maurice Green, Winifred Booker,
Daphne Boothby, Margaret Crosby, Wendy Gillett, Judi Grant, Martin Morley,
Avril and Ray Brown, Debby Mason, Sue Wood, Martin Aptisis (Tasmania),
Karol London (New Zealand), Maurice Wigham (Ireland).

Drawings from many children in several countries have been compiled to form the lower sections in a number of panels, and in these we delight.

Research into the subject matter for panels and for the text of the 1989 Guide was undertaken by Harold Nichols, Betty Harris and many of the groups concerned, with contributions also from Elfrida Vipont Foulds, Ormerod Greenwood, David Butler and Anne Wynn-Wilson. We have where necessary revised it.

The panels have been embroidered by the groups or individuals named in the Chart on pages 8-9, supervised by the Scheme's embroidery teachers:

Anne Wynn-Wilson, Ann Castle, Ann Nichols, Jill Robinson, Cathy Spence,
and, at the beginning of the project, Maggie Goodrich.

Photography is by Mr. Adrian Gale, Pershore, Worcestershire.

Production under the direction of Mr. Andrew Miller of Lithographics Ltd. of Worcester.

To all these the Committee expresses warm thanks for all their help and patience with the demands made on both their time and gifts.

Kathleen L. Cottrell
Edward H. Milligan
Margaret H.Simpson
for the Quaker Tapestry Scheme Committee

January 1992

Introduction   by Margaret H. Simpson

The Quaker Tapestry is a unified crewel embroidery of seventy-Seven separate panels that celebrate the spiritual insights that have motivated the Religious Society of Friends (Quakers) since it was founded by George Fox in 1652. The tapestry began in 1981 in the Friends Meeting in Taunton, Somerset, where Anne Wynn-Wilson was responsible for a children's class, sometimes only one boy; they met on Sundays in a gloomy room in the old part of the Meeting House. Jonathan had been hearing about the beginnings of Quakerism, about George Fox and his search for a religion he could believe in, in that period of religious and political revolution, and his amazement when, out of his despair he heard a voice that said "There is one, even Christ Jesus, that can speak to thy condition", and his heart did leap with joy! He had listened to stories of George Fox's travels through the Midlands and the North of England to tell others of his great discovery, of his meeting in Westmorland with groups of Seekers, who like him had renounced the formalism of a church worship that did not satisfy them; and of how, when he came into their meetings, a fire was kindled in their hearts that united them into the group from which the Society of Friends sprang. Here was a thrilling story that had to be illustrated, and the walls of a dreary room needed covering! Jonathan knew that Anne Wynn-Wilson was a gifted embroiderer, and he suggested that, instead of drawings, they should try to embroider pictures to tell this story.

That set her thinking. She had recently completed work for an advanced embroidery qualification that had involved a study of the Bayeux Tapestry. She was enthralled by the idea of telling stories by means of embroidery, of which that famous 11th Century Tapestry is the supreme example, and the possibility of using embroidery to tell the story of Quakerism began to fire her imagination. How the idea that started in such unpropitious surroundings has grown into the Quaker Tapestry Scheme is a story in itself, which Anne Wynn-Wilson tells in her Prologue to *The Quaker Tapestry Book: A Celebration of Insights* by John Ormerod Greenwood, published in 1990. This is a brief account to introduce the visitor to exhibitions of the fruits of that vision.

Anne's purpose was to create a craft project that could be shared between groups of Friends, young and old, in widely scattered areas of the country, from which they would learn something of the story of Quakerism, and in the course of working together, get to know one another better. She proposed a crewel embroidery of separate panels that would become a unified whole, and to this end she laid down certain guidelines. The panels were to be of a size (25"x21") that could be easily transported and accommodated on the largest embroidery frame available to the amateur. The technique was based on the Bayeux Tapestry and, like that embroidery, the design is divided laterally into three sections. The background fabric would be handwoven wool, robust enough to stand unpicking, transportation and the ravages of time. It has an easily seen regular weave, with a random stripe in the warp, which gives guidance for horizontal and vertical design work, e.g. lettering. She selected one hundred and twenty natural dye type colours from Appleton's crewel embroidery wools. Each panel would have a restricted colour scheme, but the overall colour effect would, it was hoped, flow and be harmonious. She selected stitches and techniques that would allow embroiderers of different ages and abilities to join in the work. Four ancient stitches are used – Stem, Split, Knot and Chain, and the ancient method of laying threads called Bayeux Point. The designs would, it was obvious, include a great deal of lettering, and so Anne Wynn-Wilson invented a new corded stitch, made by combining Stem and Split Stitches, which we have called Quaker Stitch. All the embroidery throughout the Tapestry is confined to these stitches, used simply or creatively, according to the skill of the worker. Detailed instructions for the embroidery techniques are described in *The Manual,* which Anne Wynn-Wilson produced first in 1982.

After some months of careful thought, Anne Wynn-Wilson presented her project to the Children & Young People's Committee of Quaker Home Service, and a grant was made that enabled her to purchase the cloth and embroidery wools. She designed the first panel, "George Fox's Convincement", and used it to test out her ideas, embroidering most of it herself but sharing the work of design and embroidery with the children in Taunton Meeting. She set up an exhibition, which included the finished panel, at the Quaker Yearly Meeting held in Warwick University in August 1982, and it immediately attracted tremendous enthusiasm. Those of us who first heard of the project through that exhibition did not fully appreciate the extent to which it would grow and dominate our lives for the next eight or nine years! The fifty panels planned initially have grown to seventyseven, and over 4,000 Friends have contributed to the work in ten countries. A membership group was formed at that Yearly Meeting, of Friends who wished to support the Scheme – there are now some 500 members: they receive a Newsletter twice a year and a free copy of *The Quaker Tapestry Calendar,* which since 1986 has been a source of essential income for the project, and a means of spreading the enthusiasm, as more and more people worldwide see the coloured reproductions of the finished panels, and read about them.

With the appointment of a Committee at that Yearly Meeting, our task was then to select sixty subjects for the panels from over four hundred suggestions received from Friends in response to our invitation. It was a difficult exercise, undertaken after much prayerful thought, and with much regret that so many favourite subjects had to be omitted. We have since ordered more fabric and added to the number, which now rests at seventyseven. Subjects were adopted by groups enthusiastic to begin work on them; first they must undertake the research needed for pictorial ideas and wording on which the design of the panel would be based. Anne received valuable help in the design of panels from Joe McCrum, and we have since been helped by several other talented artists, but our greatest problem has been to maintain the high standard and uniformity of design set by Anne Wynn-Wilson, in time to provide the cartoon for a group before its enthusiasm waned. Then workshops had to be organised to teach the techniques required to transfer the design and embroider it. Again, the help of Friends who were skilled embroiderers was offered, and our teachers have included Ann Castle, Ann Nichols, at an earlier stage Maggie Goodrich, and more recently Jill Robinson and Cathy Spence. Workshops were held in Meeting Houses, sometimes for a day and sometimes over a weekend; and we have especially enjoyed the residential weekends spent at Charney Manor and Woodbrooke (and on one occasion at Westhope College, Shropshire, and at Lattendales, near Penrith). These led to the organisation of Quaker Tapestry holiday workshops, when some sixty of us enjoyed a week together in the Lake District, in York, and at Charbonnières, France, when we visited the Bayeux Tapestry and began the contacts that led to the invitation to exhibit the Quaker Tapestry on their premises in August 1990.

One of the most exciting aspects of the Scheme has been the interest it has aroused among Friends overseas. The first panel to travel to another continent was *Elizabeth Fry and the Patchwork Quilts,* which in 1984 was taken by Ann Castle to Perth, Australia, where she worked on it under a gum tree in a temperature of 104! It was then embroidered by enthusiastic Friends of all ages in Adelaide, Melbourne, Hobart and Sydney Meetings, and returned to us completed in beautiful condition. *Quakerism in New Zealand–Aotearoa,* likewise, has travelled round that country, and come back to us with the signatures of some 200 Friends who have contributed to its embroidery. The panel commemorating *Backhouse and Walker in Van Diemen's Land* was completed in Tasmania, and *Friends in Canada* accompanied Ann and Harold Nichols on a visit to that country, where many meetings contributed to the design and embroidery. Nearer home, two panels come from Ireland, *The Great Hunger* embroidered in the south, and *Reconciliation* in the north, and the Scottish group have taken their panels *Publishers of Truth* and *Oaths* to Friends all over Scotland, from the Islands of Orkney to the South West.

Anne Wynn-Wilson was invited in 1988 to teach the Tapestry techniques at Pendle Hill, a Quaker college in Pennsylvania, and as a result we have a panel on *The Underground Railroad* designed in the USA, where Friends are now planning an American Quaker Tapestry of their own. Anne also took with her to USA *The World Family of Friends* panel, which is a truly international effort, with children's drawings in the lower border from England, Scotland, France, East Germany, Sweden, Canada, USA, Chile, Mexico and Japan, and embroidery contributed in England, Scotland, Switzerland and America.

Since the summer of 1989 there has been a continuous series of exhibitions, including those at the Aberdeen Art Gallery and Edinburgh Meeting House (1989), Royal Festival Hall and Bayeux (1990), Bristol (1991) and many other art galleries and Meeting Houses throughout Britain. A programme of exhibitions is arranged for 1992 and 1993 including, it is hoped, a number overseas. When the Tapestry has the permanent home for which we plan, it is intended that panels will continue to be available for exhibition elsewhere. The use of the embroideries to interest people who might not otherwise have known much about Quakerism has always been part of the vision that has inspired the Tapestry. Its purpose has always included not only education in Quaker history and the supportive value of group activity for Friends of all ages, but also a continuing opportunity for Quaker outreach in an unusual and imaginative way.

Since Anne Wynn-Wilson set up her exhibition at Warwick University in 1982, this exciting enterprise has caught the imagination of all who come in touch with it, and particularly those who are fortunate enough to hear about it from Anne herself. We hope that exhibitions of the completed Tapestry will enable us to share with an even wider public these stories of the spiritual insights, devotion and achievements of Friends during the past three centuries.

But if we have conveyed through the Quaker Tapestry only a story of the past, our purpose will have been unfulfilled. The Society of Friends is very much alive today as a number of the panels will, we hope, testify. And the cooperative effort which has produced the Tapestry is evidence of the many seeking, caring groups of Friends who gather together regularly, week by week, in their Meeting Houses for Quaker meeting for worship. Our aim has always been to celebrate the insights, the inspiration, the guidance, that have come to Friends through the past three centuries, and, in our experience, continue to come to us today. In the words of the late George Gorman,

> What's so amazing about Quaker worship is that for over 300 years groups of ordinary people have met together in silence, without the aids of a trained leader, or of liturgy, ritual or outward sacraments. Week by week they have shared in a corporate experiment of silent, yet open worship. In it they have felt the sense of the grandeur and tragedy of life; its defeats and triumphs. They have been aware of something overwhelming: a presence, a sense of transcendence, of truth, of the love of God. By this awareness they have been held and at the same time invigorated and re-created. So they have been drawn to make a tremendous affirmation about life's essential goodness and purpose, for they have become real people.*

The Amazing Fact of Quaker Worship (Swarthmore Lecture, 1973). George Gorman

The Quaker Tapestry Chart

Title Panel: The Prism
(Chapter 1),
Anne Wynn-Wilson &
Winifred Booker.

God and man (Chapters 1, 2, 3) A	Publishing Truth (Chapter 8) B	The Meeting (Chapters 4, 5, 6, 7, 15) C
1 George Fox's Convincement *Anne Wynn-Wilson*	1 Firbank Fell George Fox preaching *Anne Wynn-Wilson*	1 Swarthmoor Hall *Margaretta Playfair & Cambridge*
2 James Nayler *Bristol*	2 Mary Fisher *Southampton*	2 Margaret Fell *Jordans*
3 James Parnell Meeting for Sufferings *Harrow*	3 John Bright *Sidmouth*	3 Keeping the Meeting *Reading*
4 Richard Sellar *Mary Siegle & Anne Wynn-Wilson*	4 Publishers of Truth *Scotland*	4 Meeting Houses *Peripatetic*
5 The Woodhouse *Nottingham*	5 Stephen Grellet *Leicester*	5 Meeting Houses Overseas *Peripatetic*
6 John Woolman *York*	6 Woodbrooke *Cotteridge*	6 Meeting Houses in the Community *Peripatetic*
7 Conscientious Objection *Margaretta Playfair & Cambridge*	7 Services Overseas *Peripatetic*	7 Quaker Schools *Peripatetic*
8 Manchester Conference *not yet completed*	8 Quaker Peace Action Caravan *Minehead*	8 Quaker Marriage *Ann Castle & Hampshire*
9 Oaths *Scotland*		9 Quaker Pilgrimages *Margaret Crosby & North West Group*
		10 Children's Work Junior Y.M. *Colchester*
		11 The Leaveners *Cathy Spence & The Leaveners*

Final Panel: The World
Family of Friends,
Anne Wynn-Wilson,
Wyn Prior & Friends
from many countries.

The Art of Living (Chapters 9, 10, 11) D	Social Responsibilities (Chapter 12) E	National and International Responsibilities (Chapters 13, 14, 15) F	
1 Lichfield and Pendle Hill *Anne Wynn-Wilson*	1 George Fox at Ulverston: Healing *Peripatetic*	1 George Fox in Derby Goal *Margaret Gardner & Derby*	12 America and Milford Haven Meeting *Wendy Gillett & South Wales*
2 Quaker Simplicity *Ann Castle & Bournemouth & Swanage*	2 John Bellers *Daphne Boothby & Hammersmith*	2 The Penn and Meade Trial *Sevenoaks & Tunbridge Wells*	13 Quakers in Dolgellau *Ros Morley & North Wales*
3 Personal Devotion *Margaret Ainger & Oxford*	3 Bankering *Darlington*	3 Slave Trade *Liverpool* *not yet completed*	14 Quakerism in New Zealand *New Zealand*
4 Coalbrookdale *Bakewell & Sheffield*	4 Criminal Justice *Mid-Somerset*	4 Daniel Wheeler *Bradford-on-Avon*	15 Workcamps *Gloucester & Nailsworth*
5 Innocent Trades *Irene Grey & Newcastle*	5 Elizabeth Fry *Hilda Jenks & Bournville*	5 Delegation to the Czar *Mary Mason & family*	16 Peace Embassies *Lewes & Brighton*
6 Quaker Merchants *Leeds*	6 Elizabeth Fry and the Patchwork Quilts *Australia*	6 Relief Work: British Isles *Manchester*	17 Vigils For Peace *Catherine Walton & Uxbridge*
7 Railways *Leicester*	7 Adult Schools *Wellingborough*	7 Relief Work Abroad *Wellington, Somerset*	18 World Conference 1991 *Rugby* *not yet completed*
8 Quaker Botanists *The Embroidery Teachers*	8 The Great Hunger *Anna Wigham & Dublin & Waterford*	8 Friends Ambulance Unit *Sidcot Meeting*	19 Quakerism in South Africa *Hampstead & South Africa*
9 Quaker Doctors *Margaretta Playfair & Cambridge*	9 Mary Hughes *Westminster*	9 Reconcilliation *Belfast*	20 Backhouse and Walker in Van Diemen's Land *Tasmania*
10 Quaker Scientists *Winifred Booker*	10 Unemployment *Hemel Hempstead*	10 The Underground Railroad, U.S.A. *The Armitage sisters* *not yet completed*	21 Friends in Canada *Canada*
11 Industrial Welfare *Hilda Jenks & Bournville*	11 Friends Provident Institution *Maggie Goodrich & Epsom*	11 Penn and Pennsylvania *Dorking & Horsham*	22 Friends in the Netherlands 1940-45 *not yet completed*
12 Query 19: Ecology *Ann Nichols & Wokingham*	12 William Allen *Salisbury*		
	13 Scott-Bader Commonwealth *not yet completed*		

THE RELIGIOUS SOCIETY of FRIENDS "might be thought of as a prism through which the DIVINE LIGHT passes to become visible in a spectrum of many colours; many more in their richness than words alone can express" Faith + Practice.

The Prism

In designing and embroidering the Title Panel herself, Anne Wynn-Wilson was inspired by the words at the beginning of Chapter 1 of *Christian Faith and Practice in the experience of the Society of Friends*, which are quoted in the panel. In attempting to express her thoughts on this design, she quotes and writes as follows:

> To attempt to ...conduct an inquiry into Friends' beliefs is a perilous exercise. One needs to emphasize repeatedly that it is an inquiry and not a statement. The result resembles a spectrogram when the light of the sun is passed through a prism: a continuous band of light passing from the invisible ultra-violet through the full range of visible colour to the invisible infra-red, crossed by a number of defined bands which show the presence of certain elements. Not a bad analogy, perhaps, if we recognize that our inquiry is directed at the light of truth refracted through the membership of the Society.
>
> (Geoffrey Hubbard, *Quaker by Convincement*, 1974, p.68).

"Light" has always been used as a symbol of purity and knowledge. From the beginning of Quakerism, Friends' teaching was of belief in the "Inward Light", in "that of God in everyone". Early Friends could quote from St.John's gospel: "...in him was life, and the life was the light of men", ... "that was the true light, which lighteth every man that cometh into the world" (John 1:4,9). Inspiration for our present time is not that religion should primarily be social, but that religion should first be spiritual. This is represented in the design by the intrinsic nature of the spiral, extending from the origin to infinity. The creative use of colour in the embroidery speaks of happiness and goodwill, of people reflecting the light, and speaks of the coming together of many different qualities, to become greater and more vibrant than one alone. At the beginning of the project our intention was to explore Quaker history, but we soon found that we were discovering the insights which motivate Friends. We began to think of the Tapestry as a celebration of Quaker insights, certainly an exploration of the mystery that led early Quakers to call themselves the Children of Light.

Title Panel

George Fox

Quakerism had its origin in the religious and political ferment of the mid-seventeenth century. George Fox (1624-1691) grew up in Fenny Drayton, Leicestershire, a village with a puritan tradition going back to the reign of Elizabeth I. After working with a shoemaker and tending sheep, Fox left home at the age of nineteen, shocked by the failure of professing Christians to live up to their Christian standards. He travelled extensively in search of spiritual help and fellowship until in 1647, as he later recorded in his *Journal*

> ..when all my hopes in all men were gone, so that I had nothing outwardly to help me, nor could tell what to do, then, oh then, I heard a voice which said, "There is one, even Christ Jesus, that can speak to thy condition", and when I heard it my heart did leap for joy.

He had left home in 1643, the year when Parliament undertook to introduce the full rigours of presbyterianism to replace episcopacy and the Book of Common Prayer. His travels were therefore not only in a country immersed in civil war but in a country full of religious questioning. He encountered many folk who were on a like spiritual journey and his personality, ministry and great pastoral gifts drew them into an enduring fellowship. Years of his life were spent in travel and he endured eight imprisonments, during one of which – at Worcester 1673-5 – he dictated the *Journal* which, first published in 1694, is a spiritual classic.

Panel A1

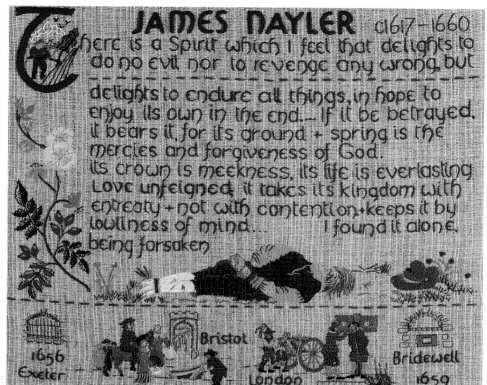

James Nayler (1617?-1660), who had been in the Parliamentary army, was some seven years older than Fox. He came from near Wakefield, Yorkshire, and from 1652 was in the forefront of the new movement, the charisma of his personality and the power of his preaching winning him golden opinions especially in London.

In 1656, travelling westward to meet Fox, then in prison at Launceston, Cornwall, Nayler was arrested and gaoled at Exeter. Fox, on release, came to Exeter but a meeting between them did credit to neither. After Nayler's release and in these tense circumstances, swayed by adulatory followers, he entered Bristol in October 1656 "acting a sign" of Christ's entry into Jerusalem. He was tried before Parliament for blasphemy and suffered extreme punishment and three years' imprisonment. The whole episode brought the infant movement into European notoriety. The ride into Bristol and his subsequent punishments are depicted in the lower part of the panel and based on illustrations from contemporary accounts.

Nayler's writings during and after imprisonment have been described as showing "a spirit of wonderful beauty". In October 1660, reconciled at last with Fox, he set forth homeward. Some miles beyond Huntingdon he was robbed and bound, and found towards evening in a field. He was taken to a Friend's house near King's Ripton, and his dying words, given more fully in *Christian Faith and Practice, 25,* form the text of this panel.

"I was at the plow, meditating on the things of God", he had said to the justices at Appleby in 1652, and this is recalled within the initial letter; while his life from spring sowing to harvest fruition is linked by the rose, symbolic of the love of God.

Panel A2

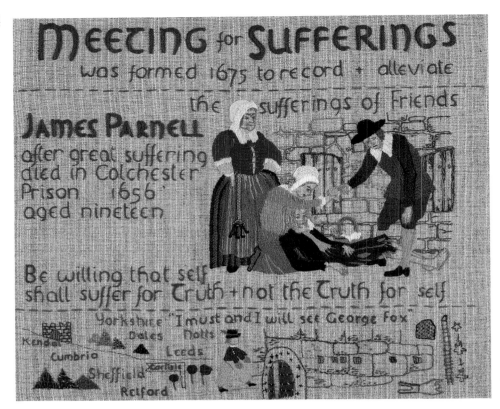

James
Parnell

James Parnell (1636-1656), became a Quaker by conviction at fifteen, and was promptly disowned by his family. After visiting Friends in the North, including, in 1653, Fox in Carlisle gaol, he preached and worked tirelessly in Cambridge and Essex. Accused of causing a riot, he was imprisoned in Colchester, being put into a high niche in the Castle wall, reached only by a ladder six feet too short, then by climbing a rope. Eventually, too weak and cold to hold the rope, he fell and was gravely injured. He was then put in a little low Hole, where he died in 1656, after eight months of imprisonment, aged only nineteen.

Though there was sporadic – sometimes severe – persecution during the Commonwealth, it became more systematic and far-reaching after the Restoration. Up to the Toleration Act 1689, about 15,000 Friends suffered various legal sentences and over 450 died in prison.

The setting up of Meeting for Sufferings, meeting weekly with an effective network of county correspondents, was in part to put a stop to those prosecutions which were in fact illegal. The Meeting's lobbying efforts on behalf of Friends in such matters as the affirmation and tithe prosecution became, in the eighteenth century, efforts on behalf of others, for example in the fight to end the slave trade.

Today Meeting for Sufferings, which is representative of Friends throughout Great Britain, meets eight or nine times a year and manages the ongoing business of the Society, discussing social and financial matters and Friends' concerns for service at home and abroad.

Panel A3

Pressed into the · Royal Prince · Scarborough 1665
RICHARD SELLAR
I was to die But no man came neither
I am at peace
with God + all men + with you my adversaries.
a mouth opened against me
I am not free to do the Kings work

Richard Sellar

Richard Sellar was a long-shore fisherman of Kilnsea, Yorkshire, who was press-ganged into the Navy in 1665 during the Second War with the Dutch. He was assigned to the flagship of Admiral Sir Edward Spragge, but he refused to serve or eat for, he said, "my warfare was spiritual and I durst not fight with carnal weapons". He was brutally beaten and lay in irons for a fortnight. Then a Council of War condemned him to death and ordered him to be hanged at the yard-arm before the captains of the Fleet. When Richard heard his sentence pronounced, he longed to rise and justify himself, but he was too weak to stand. But in utter weakness he felt God's power holding him, and a Voice said quite distinctly in his heart "Be still". Which Voice he obeyed and was comforted, and strength was given him to say to his accusers "...I do not value what you can do to this body, for I am at peace with God and all men, and with you my adversaries". At the last moment, however, the Admiral had him freed as no evidence was offered against him and he recognised Richard Sellar was a good Christian; from then on Richard served on the ship as a non-combatant. He was eventually given a free discharge.

We asked counsel of the **LORD** as the **WOODHOUSE** sailed for the New World 1657

Cut through · steer a straight course · mind nothing but **ME**

Robert Fowler thou hast her not for nothing

Contrary to my will she was brought to London where eleven friends awaited a captain willing to take them to America

The Woodhouse

Robert Fowler, a master mariner of Bridlington, Yorkshire, built *The Woodhouse* in 1657 for his own use locally, but "contrary to my will" found himself taking her to London. There he found eleven Friends awaiting passage for New England but they could find no captain willing to take them for fear of the penalties on landing.

London Friends with whom Robert Fowler conferred confirmed his reluctant conviction that he must offer his ship to convey them though, most of his crew having been pressganged, he set sail with but two men and three boys. At Portsmouth, however, he was able to secure a crew through another captain, who warned him that *he* would never undertake the voyage in so small a vessel.

Escaping from a pirate ship in a sudden mist, the Quakers sought divine help as to their course and had a sense, as Robert Fowler later described it, of "the Lord leading our vessel even as it were a man leading a horse by the head". The panel reflects this experience by depicting above the sails the hand of God, a traditional form for expressing his guidance.

After an adventurous two-month voyage in the frail barque the company landed on Long Island near New Amsterdam, a tolerant Dutch colony. The small houses to the right of the panel have as background a hint of the skyscrapers of the New York it was to become.

Panel A5

JOHN WOOLMAN 1720~1772
his beliefs went beyond religion to the guidings of Absolute Truth

"Tender compassion fills my heart toward my fellow creatures" J. Woolman

John Woolman

Eighteenth century Quakerism was in a very real sense an Atlantic community of Friends, kept alive through the visits of Friends travelling in the ministry.

John Woolman (1720-1772) was one such ministering Friend. Reflecting that "though my natural inclination was towards merchandise, yet I believed Truth required me to live more free from outward cumbers", he determined to live simply and when he was about 36 gave up merchandise altogether in favour of business as a tailor, which he could control more easily. His first religious journey in 1743 was purely local. It was the first southern journey (1746) which brought him face to face with aspects of slavery that he had not encountered in his local vicinity. There were Quakers among the slaveholders and on his second southern journey (1757) he insisted on paying his hosts, or the slaves themselves, for services rendered. It was the following year that Philadelphia Yearly Meeting took the decisive step of removing from all positions of authority all its slave–owning members, though it was not until 1776 that all Philadelphia Friends were entirely clear of slave owning.

In 1763 he visited the Indians, feeling a drawing "toward the natives of this land who dwell far back in the wilderness, whose ancestors were the owners and possessors of the land where we dwell, and who for a very small consideration assigned their inheritance to us". He went to them "that I might feel and understand their life and the spirit they live in", an attitude singularly enlightened for that time or, indeed, for later times.

In 1772 he felt a call to England. After attending Yearly Meeting in London, he went north on foot because of his concern at the cruelty shown to coach-horses. Arriving in York he developed smallpox and died at Almery Garth in Marygate, the home of Thomas and Sarah Priestman. He is remembered as a man who sought always the guidance of absolute truth.

Panel A6

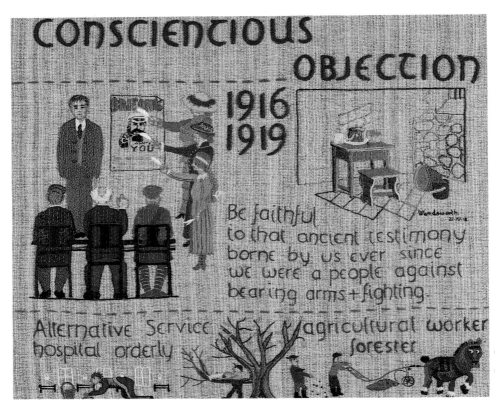

Conscientious
Objection:
1916-1919

The Society of Friends, along with the Mennonites and the Church of the Brethren, is one of the "Historic Peace Churches". Quakers suffered imprisonment under the Militia Acts of the eighteenth and nineteenth centuries. It was, however, the Military Service Act 1916 which first affected Friends – and many others – in large numbers. The tribunals set up to consider exemptions comprised local magnates and tradesmen, with a military representative: they had to consider claims on grounds of hardship or health as well as those of conscience and it is perhaps no wonder that their procedures, attitudes and decisions varied vastly from place to place. Conscientious objectors were widely regarded as cowards and many became used to being offered white feathers by belligerent women. In the first, as in the second, world war some were absolutist in their opposition to conscription, refusing to countenance any alternative service; others were prepared to accept alternative service in Quaker relief or Friends Ambulance Unit (see panels F7, F8) or, as shown here, in hospital work or on the land. Those who refused to accept the tribunal decisions or whose claims were disallowed found themselves in prison: this was their witness against conscription.

Panel A7

1895 the MANCHESTER CONFERENCE
challenged the old thinking + distressed some people.

"Friends are not bound by a heritage or creeds + need not break with their great past to put themselves in touch with the present"

John Wilhelm Rowntree. 1868-1905

God's truth is given for every age, + it is our duty to welcome the light which may just be reaching us." Frances Thompson. 1840-1920

The Manchester Conference 1895

In the latter part of the nineteenth century new scientific knowledge had disturbed the simple fundamental faith of many Friends and caused intellectual struggles. At Yearly Meeting 1893 John Wilhelm Rowntree(1868-1905) commended a new approach which could reconcile the old, satisfy the young, and bring Friends into contact with other Christians in better mutual understanding, and with more readiness to accept necessary social responsibilities.

Two years later the Manchester Conference examined thoroughly both Quakerism's inner life and its work in the world. In an inspiring speech, John Wilhelm Rowntree stated his belief that from "the present seeming chaos" would come "a renewed and more powerful faith, deeper in its basis, clearer in its vision, broader in its charity....and as warm in its love." The Society faced the issue of the day squarely and decided to go forward, admitting its members' need for study and training. This was met by the Summer School movement and the establishment in 1903 of Woodbrooke, the residential Quaker College (see Panel B6).

John Wilhelm Rowntree had when young been threatened with loss of both sight and hearing. In his moment of despair he had experienced the love of God, a love which never left him. His own youthful intellectual difficulties, which had almost caused him to resign membership, gave him understanding of and influence over other troubled souls. His life was short: but he was to express a passion for reality, for a religious life and growth which helped to rekindle the ardent flame of early Quakerism.

"**SWEAR NOT AT ALL**" matthew chapter 5 v 34

The ability to claim Burgess Rights regained Aberdeen 1714

Friend Robert Barclay reading the Act of the Privy Council.

We regard the taking of oaths as contrary to the teaching of Christ, as setting up a double standard of truthfulness, whereas sincerity and truth should be practised in all dealings of life. Christian Faith & Practice 1911 + 25

Oaths

From the outset, Quakers had seen that Truth required that they should refuse to take oaths – quoting if necessary Matthew 5: 34 and James 5: 12. The oath was a commonplace of contemporary life for a whole host of day-to-day transactions, as well as more major matters. Normal legal practice prevented those who would not swear from carrying on trade in corporate towns, proving wills involving goods and chattels, giving evidence to defend title to land, or entering numerous professions or positions of office. Tendering to a Quaker the Oath of Allegiance was always a certain way to secure a conviction.

The Affirmation Acts of 1696 and 1722 eased the position of Quakers in England and Wales to some extent. In Scotland the use of affirmation rather than oath-taking was a well established tradition, and so there were few problems compared with the situation in England and Wales.

However, Burgess Oaths in Scotland, and particularly in Aberdeen, presented other problems. The Provost and Baillies of Aberdeen inserted an additional clause in the oath worded in terms which excluded both Catholics and Quakers – burgesses had to swear, or to affirm, that they held to neither the Catholic nor Quaker faith. There were a number of prominent Quaker families in Aberdeen who had rights as burgesses (Parkers, Jaffrays and Barclays amongst others), and who were effectively disbarred. These Friends were unwilling to compromise or to lose their rights. They therefore pursued their case to the highest level, receiving a ruling from the Lord Advocate, the senior Scottish Law Officer, that a solemn affirmation was sufficient, and on 21 June 1714 obtaining an Act of the Privy Council of Great Britain, ordering the Provost and Magistrates of the City of Aberdeen to remove the offending words from the Burgess Oath. Robert Barclay II, the Apologist's son, presented this Act to the Town Council in August 1714, and fourteen Quaker burgesses were subsequently readmitted by affirmation.

Panel A9

SEDBERGH - FIRBANK FELL
PRESTON PATRICK - BRIGFLATTS - 1652
Many groups of Seekers   heard George Fox preach

Keep your feet upon the top of the mountain and sound deep to that of God in everyone.

Firbank Fell: George Fox Preaching

After journeying through the east midlands and southern and eastern Yorkshire, George Fox travelled through the West Riding of Yorkshire to Sedbergh, which he reached in June 1652 at the time of the hiring fair. He preached outside the church, depicted here, and on the following Sunday preached for some three hours on nearby Firbank Fell to about 1,000 people. There was a chapel on the fell and many worshippers "looked out of the windows and thought it a strange thing to see a man to preach on a hill or mountain and not in their church (as they called it)". But Fox declared that "Christ was come, who ended the temple, and the priests, and the tithes."

He bade the people take heed of the spirit of God in their hearts and obey its guidance in their daily lives; he told them that the spirit that inspired the Scriptures was living and working still in the hearts of men and women, ready to reveal fresh truths; and, reminding them that their bodies were the living temples of a living Lord, he called them one and all to follow Christ. At Firbank Chapel and Preston Patrick John Audland and Francis Howgill were leaders and preachers among a group known as the Westmorland Seekers, and through Fox's preaching and the experience of this Whitsun fortnight many of them were convinced of the Quaker message. From this time Quakerism became a significant movement.

Panel B1

Mary
Fisher

From the beginning women were active in bearing their "testimony for the Lord". Mary Fisher, a Yorkshire servant girl and an early convert to Quakerism, was soon in York gaol for arguing with an established minister of the church. There, with many other Quakers, she learnt to write. After being publicly scourged at Cambridge along with Elizabeth Williams and twice imprisoned, she left England with the much older Ann Austin; they were the first Friends to go to America to spread the Quaker message. They sailed first to Barbados. On arrival in Boston the next year, the authorities burned their books, arrested them, searched their bodies for witch-marks and returned them to Barbados. The Calvinists of Boston continued to persecute "the cursed sect of Quakers", and from 1658 had a death penalty if any came back after banishment. Mary Dyer of Rhode Island, reprieved once, returned and was hanged on Boston Common where her statue now stands.

Convinced that there was a seed of God in every human heart, the early Quakers travelled extensively to share their message of the universal love of God. In 1657 a party of six Friends travelled through the Mediterranean and, after divers misadventures, two or three of them, including Mary Fisher, journeyed from Zante by land, sea and land again to where the young Sultan Mohammed IV was encamped near Adrianople. He heard Mary Fisher attentively, expressing his respect for "such an one as had taken so much Pains to come to them so far as from England with a message from the Lord".

Mary was twice married: she emigrated to Charleston, South Carolina, where she died. Her work there and in Barbados was the more valuable, but her visit to the Sultan clearly illustrates the fearless obedience of early Friends to their leadings.

Panel B2

John Bright

Until the early nineteenth century the Test and Corporation Acts stood in the way of Quakers entering Parliament. The abolition of the Acts in 1828-9 enabled Friends to stand in local elections, and in 1833 Joseph Pease (1799-1872) of Darlington sat as the first Quaker MP. There have never been many Friends in either House – perhaps no more than 75 or 80 in over 150 years. We celebrate the Quaker contribution to parliamentary government in John Bright(1811-1889), a lifelong member of Rochdale Friends Meeting, Lancashire.

The power of Bright's speeches could not be ignored, and the stand he took against Britain's entry into the Crimean War made him the conscience of the House. The words quoted in the panel refer to the alliance with Turkey that drew Britain into the war. His greatest speech opposing it included the words "The Angel of Death has been abroad throughout the land, you may almost hear the beating of his wings...".

In the American Civil War (1860-1865) he supported Abraham Lincoln against the slave owners of the South, contrary to the British government's inclinations, and he acted as mediator when the crisis arose over the sailing of the *Alabama*. He resigned from the Government as a moral protest against the bombardment of Alexandria by the British fleet in 1882. The ribbons in the design record the parliamentary issues with which he was concerned.

John Bright throughout his life worshipped with Friends and identified himself with the Society. He was only the second Quaker to become a Member of Parliament, and his Quaker convictions are well expressed by his words "Force is not a remedy".

Panel B3

PUBLISHERS of TRUTH

The principal fountain of truth must be the Truth itself

Robert Barclay of Ury published his Apologia 1676

Others wrote
Journals + letters
Edward Burrough
Isaac Penington
Benjamin Clark
Mary Westwood
John Woolman
Job Scott.

Tracts were often printed by women and distributed by travelling ministers and packmen

Publishers
of Truth

With Swarthmoor Hall as a base, a group of Friends, the "First Publishers of Truth", took their Quaker message throughout Britain and Ireland, and overseas (see panel Cl).

"Let all nations hear the word by sound or writing" wrote George Fox from Launceston Gaol in 1656. This panel commemorates those "First Publishers of Truth" and those of later generations, like the saintly American Friends John Woolman and Job Scott, who wrote tracts or books in their lifetimes or whose journals were published after their deaths. It also commemorates Quaker printers such as Mary Westwood, who was printing as early as 1658, and Benjamin Clark, whose imprint is on Jacob Claus's edition of Barclay's *Apologia.*

Robert Barclay (1648-1690) of Ury, Scotland, became a Friend in the 1650s. Educated in Paris, he had a rigorous theological training, and at twenty-seven wrote his famous *Apology,* the first major work to expound Quakerism in theological language.

Printing presses were authorised only in London, Oxford and Cambridge. State policy was executed through Stationers' Hall, where books were registered, and the Star Chamber exercised censorship. Friends' prolific tracts could, therefore, be printed only in secret and illegally, until in 1695 the Licensing Act lapsed.

By 1700 some 4000 publications had emerged from the Quaker press, ranging from single sheets to "collected works" of 500 pages or more. The Orkney wagon, its bright cover made from re-used sailcloth from fishing boats, is a reminder that there were few places untouched, at one time or another, by the Quaker printed word.

Panel B4

STEPHEN GRELLET 1773-1855
Proclaim unto others what the Lord has done for thy soul
l'Evangile tomba sur eux comme la rosée sur la nouvelle herbe

Stephen Grellet

A French aristocrat who fled the Revolution first to South America and then to the United States, Stephen Grellet (1773-1855) became a convinced Quaker, a great traveller and an impressive preacher. He made three extensive visits to Europe, during one of which he went into Newgate prison and, immediately afterwards, visited Elizabeth Fry saying that "something must be done immediately for those poor suffering children", so initiating her work for prisoners (see panels E5 and E6).

The panel depicts, on the left, Czar Alexander I of Russia, whom he visited in 1818 with William Allen (see Panel E11) and, on the right, the aged Pope Pius VII, whom he visited at the end of the following year. In front on the right a Jewish rabbi, a prisoner in chains and a ragged woman serve as reminders that Stephen Grellet met all with an equal and sensitive concern. His preaching was so compelling that (as illustrated by the children) his listeners in a French orchard once hung lamps in the trees to prolong their meeting with him into the night.

The centre shows Grellet alone in front of a hut. The story goes that he once felt called to visit a lumber camp in the distant forest. He found his way to it, but the lumberjacks had left for a new working site. The driving force which called him to the place would not be satisfied until he had offered his ministry in an empty dining shanty. Years later on one of his many visits to Europe, he was stopped by a stranger in London who asked if he had ever preached at a lumber camp in America. He said he had, but there had been no-one present. The stranger told him that he had heard his ministry, having returned for his tools, and listened through a crack in the timber walls to the man "preaching to nobody"! The lumberjack had been converted and became a missionary. This story has no firm foundation and may derive from a mis-remembering of another and less dramatic story which Stephen Grellet once recounted. Yet it so well illustrates his sensitivity to divine leading that it has a fitting place in the centre of the panel.

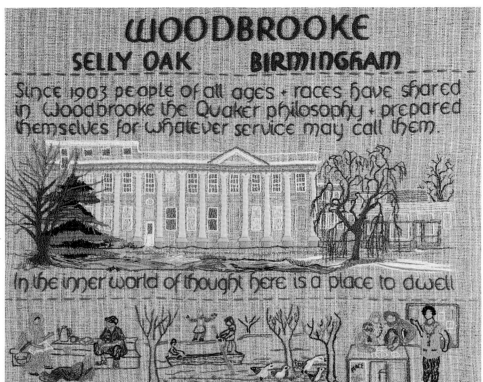

Woodbrooke

In 1897 some 700 British and Irish Quakers attended a summer school at Scarborough. World experts introduced sessions on Biblical history and criticism and the responsibilities of Christians in relation to social and international problems. Other smaller, more local, summer schools and settlements followed, and a growing awareness of need led to an article, "A plea for a permanent settlement". The plea was answered through George Cadbury's gift of Woodbrooke, hitherto his Birmingham home, but opened in 1903 as the first of a group of Selly Oak Colleges.

Nowadays, the Woodbrooke curriculum is broadly based, covering religious, social, international and cultural themes. Though Woodbrooke is integral to the Selly Oak Colleges, it remains an independent, international Quaker adult religious education college. It offers full-term residential courses, short courses, staff to lead "On the road" extra-mural courses, and study materials.

Thus Woodbrooke continues to prove a meeting point for students of many faiths and races, as well as ages, whether for a year, a term, a few weeks or a few days, in a diverse life centred round daily worship. In this lovely house on the edge of Birmingham, set among trees and with a lake in the grounds, friends are made, knowledge widened, skills nurtured; and here change and growth may take place.

Panel B6

Service Overseas

The Friends' Foreign Mission Association was set up in 1868 to assist those Friends who heeded the call to spread the Gospel abroad. From the beginning education and medical assistance went together with ministry, and nowhere was this more successful than in China. The left centre of the panel shows a boat working its way along the Yangtze Kiang, among mountains and through gorges where it would be manhandled by "trackers" pulling bamboo ropes. This was the way the FFMA missionaries travelled from Shanghai to Szechwan, then overland to Chengdu. Here they cooperated with other Christian missions in founding the West China Union University (1910): the buildings were designed by the Quaker architect Fred Rowntree, and one is shown in this panel. It is now the West China University of Medical Sciences.

From 1897 Friends were concerned to show, at Friends Industrial Mission, Pemba, how plantations could be run with free labour, half the island's people having been enslaved until a few years before: this work is recalled on the right of the panel.

"Helping people help themselves" has long been an objective in all Quaker development work, and this is illustrated in the centre of the panel by the efforts to improve the garden produce of Ethiopian refugees in Somalia; while the left hand of the lower section shows a Salvadorean refugee being taught carpentry skills.

The right of the lower section shows the use of a series of specially devised concrete rings to sink wells in central India and thus to help irrigation and better crops.

Panel B7

Q-PAC MAY 1980

Campaigning for a less violent world

QUAKER **PEACE ACTION** CARAVAN

IN SCHOOLS IN THE STREET AND IN THE PEACE MOVEMENT

World Peace will only come through action by ordinary people like yourself

Choose LIFE

Quaker Peace Action Caravan

It was in May 1980 that the Quaker Peace Action Caravan (the vision of Barry and Jill Wilsher) began its extensive travels, which continued until the end of 1985. It was a short-lived piece of work but one which touched the imaginations – and the lives – of many British and Irish Quakers as well as of many others.

It described itself as "a mobile resource for peace education". The message which the van, and the panel, convey, that of working for a less violent world, is a reminder that violence is anything which damages, degrades or destroys human beings, and the Q-PAC team explored with those they met the connections between the violence we do to each other in our everyday lives, the violence in the community in which we live, and the global violence which threatens the existence of the human race and of our planet.

Whether in street theatre, work in schools or putting new heart into tired and dispirited peace workers, it is always the individual encounter which is important. The message of Q-PAC was always, as the message at the foot of the panel makes clear, that individuals are not helpless but can in the long run change things.

Panel B8

Swarthmoor Hall

The arrival in summer 1652 of George Fox, James Nayler and Richard Farnworth at Swarthmoor Hall, near Ulverston, in the Furness district of Lancashire, was to prove of first importance for the next half-century of Quakerism. Swarthmoor was the home of Thomas and Margaret Fell and their growing family. Thomas Fell was a circuit judge and, though he never became a Quaker, offered the Hall as a place for Friends to worship in – no light gesture. It was used for meetings for worship until 1688 when a meeting house was built nearby.

Until the death of Margaret Fell in 1702 the Hall was an administrative and pastoral centre for Friends. From 1654 onwards the "First Publishers of Truth" or "Valiant Sixty" – mainly from this part of England – travelled to the south of England, to the continent of Europe and to America with the Quaker message. Among members of the Swarthmoor household were Thomas Salthouse, who laboured chiefly in the south-west of England, Anne Clayton, who travelled to Barbados and America, and William Caton, who became the apostle of Quakerism in Holland.

Swarthmoor Hall, which had been long out of Quaker hands, is now the property of London Yearly Meeting, and is open to visitors for much of the year.

Panel C1

Margaret Fell

The driving energy, administrative flair and social position of Margaret Fell (1614-1702) made an immense impact on the first fifty years of Quakerism. On ten occasions, the last when she was 84 years old, she visited London – a journey there and back of over 500 miles.   In June 1660, when Fox was imprisoned in Lancaster, accused of plotting against the newly-restored king, she delivered into Charles II's hands a declaration on the peaceable nature of Friends' witness. She was accompanied by Ann Curtis, daughter of a former sheriff of Bristol who was hanged for his loyalty to Charles I.

Margaret Fell's seven daughters all married Friends but her son George was antagonistic to Quakerism and, after Judge Fell's death in 1658, made various attempts to wrest the Swarthmoor estate from his mother. He was involved in the events leading to her 1664 arrest, trial and imprisonment under sentence of *Praemunire* – which placed her outside the king's protection and involved forfeiture of goods and chattels, loss of all income from real property, and imprisonment for life at the king's pleasure.

She was, in the event, released in June 1668: she had written several pamphlets while in prison, including *Women's speaking justified,* a defence of the vocal ministry of women.

In 1669, eleven years after Judge Fell's death, she married George Fox: though her daughters and sons-in-law offered warm support, her son George, as depicted here by the children, was discontented and absent.

Panel C2

KEEP YOUR MEETINGS

... for they might as well think to hinder the sun from shining or the tide from flowing as to think to hinder the Lord's people from meeting to wait upon him.

Horslydown Meeting 1670 demolished by order of the King

The children kept the Meeting when the law forbade their parents to forgather 1662

Keeping the Meeting

Quakers met (and in the "unprogrammed" tradition still meet) for worship in silent expectant waiting, believing that out of that silence the ministry of the word may be given to any one of the worshippers, man or woman. The Quaker Act 1662 made it an offence for Quakers to assemble, five or more, under the pretence or colour of worship not authorised by law. The Conventicle Act 1664 was the Quaker Act stiffened and extended to all nonconformists, and the Conventicle Act 1670 gave sweeping powers (and profits) to the common informer. That year Christopher Wren, King's Surveyor, was directed to destroy the meeting-house at Horslydown; "a party of soldiers came with carpenters and pulled down the meeting-house and carried away the boards, windows, benches and forms, and sold them". Friends met next day upon the rubble until dragged off by soldiers. They were constant in their attendance for six months before they were left in peace. The 1689 Toleration Act gave dissenters a degree of freedom of conscience.

In Reading and Bristol in particular the children kept up the meeting when the adult Friends were in gaol and, despite beatings and whippings by the authorities, continued "with a remarkable Gravity and Composure". Richard Baxter (no friend to Quakers) wrote that "many turned Quaker, because the Quakers kept their meetings openly and went to prison for it cheerfully".

The gathered meeting is the heart of the

MEETING HOUSE

Come with heart & mind prepared

Meeting
Houses

Early Quakers met to worship wherever it was convenient, whether it was in the Great Hall at Swarthmoor (see Panel Cl) or in a farmhouse kitchen, or, less comfortably, "they met without Doors, for many years, on a place called Pardshow Cragg". But the need for "a place of one's own" gradually led to the building of meeting houses or the adaptation of existing buildings. The extreme simplicity of earlier meeting houses gave way to more elaborate buildings in the later 18th and 19th centuries, while 20th century meeting houses have again tried to meet changing needs.

At the top of the panel are Mount Street, Manchester (1830), Jordans (1688), Hertford (1670), Broad Campden (1663) and Burlington, New Jersey (1686), with, behind it, Blackheath (1972). In the middle are, to the left, Swarthmoor Hall, and then – with Friends House, London (1926) as a background – Come-to-Good, Cornwall (1709), Brigflatts (1675) and Drapers, Margate (1740). At Burlington, New Jersey, the shape of the Abbot's Kitchen at Glastonbury, Somerset, was copied because Friends had been meeting there before they left England.

While, out of the gathered silence, any of the worshippers might – and may – speak, it was early recognised that to some the ministry of the word was entrusted in larger measure than to others: these Friends, men and women, became known as recorded ministers. They, with the elders, who had responsibility for the spiritual life of the meeting, sat on raised benches at one end of the meeting house. A separate room was usually provided for women Friends to conduct their business meetings. From the late 19th century all business meetings have been conducted jointly, and the 20th century saw the gradual discontinuance of the ministers' and elders' gallery or stand.

Meeting Houses are sometimes no longer needed, as happened at Broad Campden. In 1930 the unused building was sold and became derelict. Bought back and restored by Charles Tyson between 1961 and 1964, the small building of Cotswold stone once more became lovely and fit for use. This panel was partly embroidered there.

Panel C4

MEETING HOUSES OVERSEAS

Norway · France · New Zealand · S Africa · Lebanon · Germany · Australia · Bolivia · Ghana · Pemba

"We met together in the unity of the Spirit, and of the bond of peace... And holy resolutions were kindled in our hearts as a fire which the Life kindled in us to serve the Lord while we had a being." Francis Howgill 1672

Meeting Houses Overseas

In 1654 the Quaker movement spread from the north of England to London and the southern counties, to the continent of Europe and to the islands of the West Indies. Only in North America did it take firm and enduring root. In the late eighteenth and nineteenth centuries srnall companies of folk who had independently reached convictions closely akin to those of Quakers were "discovered" by travelling Friends: these groups are commemorated by the meeting houses at Congenies in the south of France, at Bad Pyrmont, Germany, and at Botn in Roldal, Norway. In all cases these groups died out, emigration being a major cause, particularly the Roldal Quakers who settled in Iowa. With the re-emergence of German Quakerism after the first world war, the meeting house at Bad Pyrmont was restored to use. In the Lebanon is the school founded by Friends at Brummana, with at its gates the Meeting House built in 1887.

Nineteenth century emigration resulted in small groups of Friends in Australia, New Zealand and, later, South Africa, represented by meeting houses in Adelaide (the building was sent out by London Friends in sixtynine packages in 1839), Auckland (1890) and Cape Town (1920) respectively. Missionary work by American Friends resulted in substantial groups in South America, notably Bolivia and Peru, while work by British Friends among the released slaves in Pemba in the 1890s led to the establishment of meetings there. The meeting at Hill House, Ghana, grew substantially after the second world war. No attempt has been made to depict the great variety of styles of meeting houses on the North American continent.

Meeting Houses in the Community

Though early meeting houses were used for schools (see Panel C7) and in the nineteenth century were used on occasion in emergency (see Panel F6) or for adult schools (see Panel E7), the twentieth century has shown a far wider use of them, and a 1944 report, *The Society of Friends and Social Service* envisaged "a greater unity between the religious service of our meetlngs and the social service of Friends, each being complementary to the other, since they are rooted in the same life and spirit".

This panel shows seven meeting houses used in a variety of ways. The top depicts Mosedale, Cumbria (1702), long closed but re-opened as a cafe for Lake District visitors, and a place of outreach, and Brighton (1805), which houses a wide-ranging Adult Education Centre where horizons are widened and doors of the mind opened. Below these are Leeds (1987) where the new meeting house is partly shared by Age Concern, and Sidcot (remodelled 1926) which adjoins the school and is as much school hall as meeting house.

Below these are Winchester where the meeting chose in 1974 to buy premises to meet local needs as well as their own, and now offer a number of services including a hostel, and Wisbech (1854), where space within the building has been adapted for sheltered housing for the elderly.

These each illustrate a single large concern. Every meeting, however, gives house-room to a variety of small local activities. Bury St.Edmunds (1750) stands here for all of these, and their children have drawn some of the activities within the local community that go on there.

Panel C6

QUAKER SCHOOLS
set up to instruct in whatsoever things were civil and useful in creation

Early schools were held in meetinghouses.

Quaker Schools

Education has from the very beginning been an essential part of Quakerism, in order that all may read and understand the Bible and Quaker writings, and manage their own affairs in the world. As early as 1668 George Fox was urging the foundation of schools for boys and girls.

Many meetings throughout the country set up such schools, some not restricted to Quaker children. Some were intermittent, others flourished to outgrow the meeting house. Most were held in the women's meeting room, where there was often a fireplace. A room might be built for the purpose, as at Brigflatts in 1709.

In addition to these "meeting schools" there were numerous "private schools", usually conducted by individual Friends: some 18th and 19th century schools like that at Compton, Dorset, or Ballitore, County Kildare (where Edmund Burke was a pupil) were widely known, while others were small and mainly restricted to Quaker children.

In the later eighteenth century the "meeting schools" became more difficult to sustain and the concern of the Yearly Meeting for education, and the zeal of a few especially concerned Friends, led to the development of the "committee schools" catering for a larger number of pupils and with a sounder basis of continued government. There are now eight of these in England and two in Ireland, all represented on this panel.

On the back row are The Mount, York (1857, formerly Castlegate, 1831); Lisburn, County Antrim (1774); Ackworth, near Pontefract (1779); Bootham, York (1846, formerly Lawrence Street, 1823) where the John Bright Library is depicted; and Sibford, near Banbury (1842). In front are Ayton, near Middlesborough (1841); Saffron Walden, Essex (1879, formerly Croydon, 1825, before that Islington Road, 1786, and established as Clerkenwell Workhouse, 1702); Newtown, Waterford (1798); Leighton Park, Reading (1890); and Sidcot, Avon (1808).

Panel C7

Seek to know one another in the things that
MARRIAGE are eternal

Friends. I take this my friend to be my wife
promising with God's help to be unto her a
loving and faithful
husband so long as we
both shall live

CERTIFICATE
OF MARRIAGE

We sensibly felt the Lord with us and
joining us, the sense whereof remained
with us all our life
Thomas・Mary Ellwood 1669

Quaker Marriage

A Quaker marriage is solemnised in an especially appointed meeting for worship during which the couple make declarations, as shown in this panel. These declarations are in essence, though not exact wording, the same as those used from the 1650s onwards. Quakers were at pains to demonstrate the care they took over preliminary enquiries and though, with the Restoration, the Church regarded Quaker marriages as invalid, they were upheld as good marriages in successive cases in the civil courts. In Lord Hardwicke's Act 1753 Quakers and Jews were exempt from the provision that all marriages must be celebrated in the parish church (Meeting for Sufferings had been vigilant on behalf of Friends). The Marriage Act 1836 and subsequent legislation for England & Wales continued to recognise and provide for the distinct nature of Quaker marriage procedure and witness.

Friends were anxious to ensure not only careful preliminaries and an open ceremony but an efficient system of registration. They early developed not only register books but a certificate reciting the details of the parties and the words of declaration, which was signed by all those present as a confirmation of the marriage. This certificate is still an essential part of Quaker procedure and the care of Friends' marriages is entrusted to a registering officer appointed by each area meeting for business: neither the presence of the superintendent registrar nor the appointment of an authorised person is necessary.

Until 1860 it was not legally possible for a Quaker to marry a non-Friend according to Friends' usage and those who "countenanced the hireling priest" by marriage in church were normally disowned. Legislation in 1860 and 1872 has enabled those who are not Friends to be married in Quaker meetings subject to approval on behalf of the area business meeting.

This panel depicts a 19th century Quaker marriage derived from a painting long popular in the Society. It serves as a reminder of George Fox's words: " We marry none. It is the Lord's work, and we are but witnesses".

Panel C8

QUAKER PILGRIMAGES

who knows on what far mountain
of the spirit a vision awaits us

the Kingdom of Heaven
did gather us
and catch us all as in a net
We came to know
a place to stand in and what to wait in

Quaker Pilgrimages

Although "Truth first sprang up in Leicestershire" and it was in the east midlands that George Fox first found companies of like-minded folk, it was in north-west England, around Sedbergh and Preston Patrick (see Panel Bl) and Swarthmoor (see Panels C1, C2) that, from that Whitsun fortnight of 1652, the movement gathered momentum and significance. A nineteenth century historian referred to it as "the Galilee of Quakerism". The George Fox tercentenary commemorations of 1924 aroused renewed interest in the area and from the 1930s there were regular expeditions to the area by senior pupils of Bootham and The Mount; this practice has grown until today all the Friends' schools enjoy this same opportunity. The 1952 Tercentenary Commemoration, which brought to the north-west Friends from all parts of the world, provided a fresh impetus, and Quaker Pilgrimages for adults and young people are now a regular feature of Quaker service in the area.

The centre of the panel depicts a group crossing the "dangerous sands" of Morecambe Bay, under supervision of the official Duchy of Lancaster guide: this was the old route from Lancaster to the Furness district and thus to Swarthmoor. Above is a reminder of Pendle Hill while below a group of "pilgrims" relax at the end of the day at the Old School, Yealand Conyers.

Panel C9

Watch with Christian tenderness over the opening minds of your **CHILDREN**

Through example and training help them to recognise the voice of God in their hearts.

Advice II.

Children's Work and Junior Yearly Meeting

At times during the 1660s the children of Reading, of Bristol and of Cambridge Meetings kept up their meetings when all grown-ups over 16 were in prison: nor were they left unmolested as they did so. And until well into the 20th century children sat throughout meetings for worship along with their elders.

But during the 1920s there was a growing movement for children to have gatherings of their own, either before or after spending a short time in the meeting for worship. A wide variety of activities is possible, depending on the age range of the children and the aptitudes of the adults who take charge of them. The Quaker Tapestry itself developed in a small meeting from the interest of one boy in stories of Quaker history. Drawings by children have been used in it, and some children have taken part in the embroidery: for instance, in Panel A5, *The Woodhouse*, a different child worked each fish.

Junior Yearly Meeting caters for those in their later 'teens; an annual gathering lasts several days, where those attending get to know contemporaries from across the country: there are talks, discussions, meetings for worship, games, music, etc.; the whole occasion is designed to interest, to instruct and to develop an awareness of the nature and purpose of the religious community of which they are an essential part. As London Yearly Meeting said in 1940, "The Society of Friends may be compared to a family of which the young children are as much members as their parents and in which all, down to the youngest, can and may bear their rightful share in the family life and interests."

Panel C10

**The
Leaveners
(incomplete)**

"The Leaveners" is an affectionate nickname for those involved in a range of Quaker Youth Arts Projects which, though run in a Friendly style, are open to anyone to join. The whole venture was initiated when the *Quaker Youth Theatre* was founded in 1978 after a street theatre festival in Lancaster. Young Friends were keen both to leaven Quakerism and dispel the illusion that Friends see no place for the arts, celebration and laughter in their lives, and also to reach out beyond the Society to speak of Quaker insights with a new voice, often that of song. All projects are highly intensive, working from dawn to midnight, and are characterised by their openness, high spirits and energy.

The Quaker Youth Theatre also works with a group of Protestant and Catholic Irish young volunteers each summer, presenting a children's theatre-workshop performance and playscheme in Derry, Northern Ireland. A youth theatre exchange began in 1988 with a group from this country visiting the USSR, and a reciprocal visit was made by eighteen young people and four adults from Russia to Aberdeen during Yearly Meeting in July/August 1989.

The Quaker Festival Orchestra and Chorus were launched in 1985, International Youth Year, when Tony Biggin's specially commissioned choral drama "The Gates of Greenham" was premiered at the Royal Festival Hall. Their second oratorio "Cry of the Earth" was performed there on Easter Monday 1990, coinciding with the Quaker Tapestry exhibition held in the Hall. *LEAP* (The Leaveners Experimental Arts Project) is another exciting development, linking a concern for youth unemployment with the development of practical skills in conflict resolution and community arts.

THE LAB (The Leaveners Arts Base) was opened in 1985 to explore the participatory arts, sparking deep experiences that fuse new friendships and quicken the spirit. Their concern is to raise consciousness about non-violence, social justice and integrity of creation through the ways of affirmation.

Panel C11

"TURN from DARKNESS to LIGHT + know the SPIRIT of GOD in your heart" G.Fox.

Repent. Rethink.

"Be still + cool in thy own mind"

"I saw an ocean of darkness + death, but an infinite ocean of light + love, which flowed over the ocean of darkness."

Woe to the Bloody City of Lichfield

Lichfield and Pendle Hill

Walking towards Lichfield in 1650, George Fox sees the Cathedral spires, one of them damaged in the Civil War and not yet replaced. The sight of the Cathedral, he says in his *Journal,* "struck at my life", and he is roused to a state of spiritual exaltation. He hears a command to go shoeless because it is holy ground. He is inspired to run through the streets crying "Woe unto the bloody city of Lichfield!", and the ground appears to be running with blood.

Fox was but lately freed from Derby Gaol, where he had suffered physically from foul prison conditions and mentally by the sight of men and women being put to death for offences like theft. He was steeped in the Bible, his mind full of its language and images: now, released at the beginning of winter after almost a year in prison, and with lowered physical vitality and heightened sensitivity of mind, his horror at man's behaviour to his brother man floods out in his cry. He had every reason to know that Joyce Lewis, who came from Mancetter, the village where he had been apprenticed, had been burned at Lichfield in the Marian persecutions in 1557, and later he heard the tradition that Christians had been martyred there under Roman rule. He sensed the terror of the past around him, and responded to it.

Two years later on Pendle Hill, Fox had a vision of "a great people to be gathered", and this is represented to the right of the panel, by the crowd of present-day Friends. Light is the theme of George Fox's ministry – the "infinite ocean of light and love which flowed over the ocean of darkness" – the light which is that of God in everyone. This panel celebrates that Light.

Panel Dl

QUAKER SIMPLICITY in all things both spiritual + material 1761

King George III asked to watch the Lord Mayor's Procession from the home of David Barclay

that the simplicity of truth may not wear out or be lost in our days nor in posterity, avoid pride and immodesty in apparel and all vain and superfluous fashions of the world. Yearly Meeting Epistle 1691

Quaker Simplicity

George Fox's *Journal* records an "opening" in 1648: "The Lord...forbade me to put off my hat to any, high or low; and I was required to 'thee' and 'thou' all men and women, without any respect to rich or poor, great or small". This was in an age when everyone was expected to know their place in the social hierarchy and behave accordingly.

The testimony to simplicity aimed to conquer the pride of possession, but it was also an economic witness in an unjust society: "The trimmings of the vain world", wrote William Penn, "would clothe the naked one". But simplicity tended to become uniformity, and Margaret Fell in her late eighties wrote against Friends "minding altogether outward things, neglecting the work of Almighty God in our hearts". She continued with some irritation – "We must look at no colours, nor make anything that is changeable colours as the hills are, nor sell them, nor wear them: but we must be all in one dress and one colour: this is a silly poor Gospel. It is more fit for us to be covered with God's Eternal Spirit, and clothed with his Eternal Light."

This panel depicts a room in the substantial Cheapside house of David Barclay (1682-1769), a wealthy London export merchant and son of Robert Barclay of the *Apologia* (see Panel B4). It was a vantage point for watching the Lord Mayor's procession and in 1761 George III asked Barclay to be his host, letting it be known that he understood Quaker scruples and did not expect any of the family to kneel when presented. As the panel shows, the men kept their hats on; the girls had been forbidden to curtsey. Queen Charlotte's dress drove one of Barclay's daughters into raptures, plain Quaker though she was. A century later most British Quakers had begun to abandon thee and thou, poke bonnet and broad brimmed hat, recognising that simplicity depends not on outward uniformity but on an uncluttered, resilient and unselfconscious attitude to life.

Panel D2

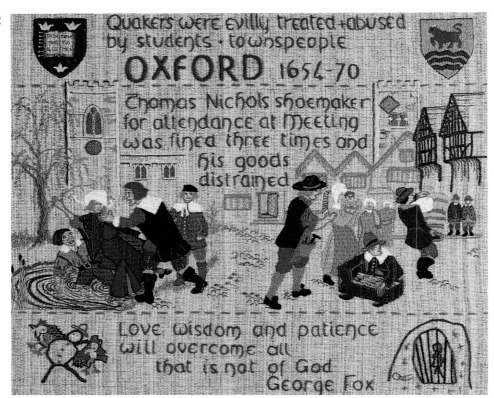

Quakers were evilly treated + abused by students + townspeople
OXFORD 1654-70
Thomas Nichols shoemaker for attendance at Meeting was fined three times and his goods distrained

Love wisdom and patience will overcome all that is not of God
George Fox

Personal Devotion

As the Quaker movement grew from its beginnings in the North of England, preachers walked South to be "valiant for the truth". In 1654 two Quaker "missionaries" arrived in Oxford and were abused by townspeople and scholars alike, being thrown into St. Giles' Pool (almost opposite the present Meeting House). Convictions for vagrancy or causing riots, imprisonment, the stocks or flogging were common, but the Quaker message was heard. The Mayor of Oxford intervened on behalf of the new Quakers, holding a meeting at his own house, and later that year a regular Meeting was started in a surgeon's house in the lane of the Seven Deadly Sins (New Inn Hall Street).

The story of Thomas Nichols, shoemaker, illustrates the period. He lived opposite Jesus College, and was convicted and imprisoned many times for not swearing the oath of allegiance, and for not attending church. In 1670, for attending Meeting, all his goods and furniture were confiscated, even the baby's pillow. He continued to attend Meeting, suffering further fines and imprisonment until 1686, when James II issued a warrant for the release of Friends in prison.

Panel D3

Coalbrookdale

Abraham Darby I (1678-1717) was a Bristol brass-founder before he bought a derelict blast-furnace and started an iron foundry in Coalbrookdale, Shropshire, in 1708. He became successful using coke for smelting as a superior fuel to charcoal. Good management was probably a key to success, but Quaker principles which made him eschew the common foundry products, armaments, led him to develop a market in domestic utensils. Darby coal mines supplied coke and the Severn provided water and transport. At his death his son was a child, and the Coalbrookdale Company was formed by his widow in partnership . Abraham II (1711-1763) continued innovation, introducing steam engines to pump the water supply. On his death the third Abraham was only 11 years old, and the manager, Richard Reynolds (1735-1816), ran the company. He was also a Quaker from Bristol, and he married Abraham II's daughter. To improve the waggon-ways and create a new product, he introduced iron rails for the first time in 1767.

Abraham III (1750-1789) made the most memorable contribution by erecting in 1781 the first cast-iron bridge: it still spans the Severn at Ironbridge. A new era had begun for civil engineering. Richard Reynolds' son, William (1758-1803), designed an inclined plane for lifting canal barges where normal locks were not possible.

John Wilkinson (1728-1808) of Broseley is also commemorated in the panel as a reminder that he took shares in the promotion of the iron bridge and of the price agreement between his non-Quaker New Willey Company and the Quaker Coalbrookdale Company.

Within the encompassing arch of the bridge are the buildings and furnaces symbolic of the life of the valley, dominated by (as Hannah Darby wrote in 1753) "the stupendous Bellows whose alternate roars, like the foaming billows, is awful to hear; the mighty Cylinders, the wheels that carry on so many different Branches of the work, is curious to observe".

Panel D4

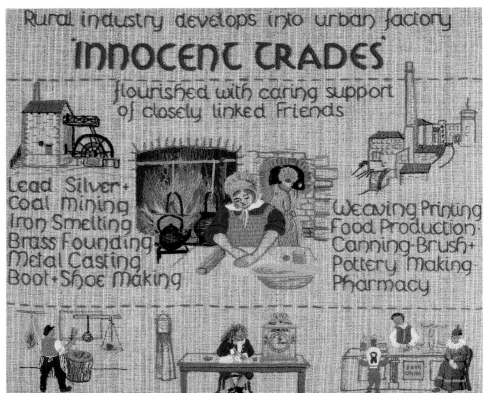

Innocent
Trades

Quaker testimony to simplicity meant that those going into trade could not manufacture superfluities. Quaker testimony against all war meant that Quaker ironmasters could not manufacture cannon. Friends were counselled to engage in "innocent trades". But Quakers testified also against covetousness, and in this sense too, trade had to be innocent. Stephen Crisp of Colchester wrote in 1680: "Take heed of enlarging your trades and traffics beyond your ability and beyond your capacity; for both these evils have been the ruin of some". Nevertheless, Quaker refusal to haggle, insisting on fixed prices, gave the public confidence in them and their businesses prospered. Most Friends avoided the consequent temptation to stylishness of living and used their brains and their money to devise and put into practice new methods and new inventions.

This panel commemorates, at the foot, Luke Cock (1657-1740), a butcher of Staithes, Yorkshire, whose convincement to Quakerism brought with it the conviction that he could no longer "swear and lie too for gain"; Daniel Quare (1648-1724), clockmaker, inventor of a repeating movement for watches, who refused a royal pension as the King's watch maker because he could not in conscience swear an oath; and a grocer to symbolise those many Quakers whose livelihood this was, not least Mary Tuke (1675-1752) of York, whose long battle with the all-powerful Merchant Adventurers Company eventually secured her the right to trade – an example of Quaker persistence.

The trades listed are a reminder of how many more names might be mentioned – the London Lead Company was for many years Quaker-owned; the Lloyd family were in the iron business before starting a bank; William Cookworthy, apprenticed as an apothecary, discovered the use of china clay and founded an industry; Ransome's made ploughs and Clark's made shoes; brewing, an earlier, prominent Quaker activity, lost its "innocent trade" appeal in Victorian times, but Friends became associated with food manufacturing – in cocoa and chocolate, Fry's, Rowntree's and Cadbury's; and in biscuits, Jacob's and Huntley & Palmer's.

Panel D5

Not slothful in business: fervent in spirit: serving the Lord.

QUAKER MERCHANTS Romans XII vii

Diligent in the management of their trades + affairs Keeping their word + promises they gained credit in the country

Gervase Elam+sons
John Gurney
John Hustler
Newman Cash

Skipton
Blackburn Burnley Bradford Leeds
Liverpool Leeds + Liverpool Canal 1770

Quaker Merchants

Along with the agriculturalists and the industrialists are the merchants. This panel concentrates on some of the many Friends engaged in the woollen trade. Before the factory system, cloth was made in the hand-loom weaver's cottage, built with wide upper-floor windows. Clothiers distributed the raw materials and collected the undyed cloth by packhorse, to take for finishing and for sale in markets of the West country, East Anglia and Yorkshire. John Gurney (1688-1741) of Norwich was known as "The weaver's advocate". By the eighteenth century, Yorkshire towns had Cloth Halls, in Leeds the White and Coloured Cloth Halls. Gervas Elam (1681-1771) of Leeds was a clothier with several wool merchant sons who had a large trade with the Americas. Many younger sons of West Riding Quaker wool merchants acted as American agents, and could stay in New York at a boarding-house run by a Quaker Yorkshirewoman. Cloth was exported to North America via Hull, but with the building of the Leeds and Liverpool Canal, it could be carried more cheaply to Liverpool. The canal was promoted by John Hustler (1715-1790), Quaker wool merchant of Bradford.

Numerous Quaker names became familiar business names, quite a number developing as banks, financial houses, shipping companies, and promoters of railways, from capital earned as wool or linen merchants.

Panel D6

Railways

In 1821 the Stockton & Darlington Railway Bill was at long last enacted. Just at this moment the engineer George Stephenson and the Quaker Edward Pease met and Stephenson was able to persuade Pease to run the line with his new steam engines. The line was opened on 27 September 1825, and the panel recalls contemporary prints of the first train crossing Skerne Bridge, Darlington (the prints are also recalled on the 1990 English £5 note). Pease was fortunate in securing the services of Stephenson, perhaps the foremost engineer of the day, who had grown affluent from extreme poverty; he is depicted sewing buttonholes to augment the slender finances of his youth.

At the foot of the panel five individuals or firms are commemorated. John Wilkinson (1728-1808), the ironmaster and railmaker, like Stephenson, was not a Quaker but without their expertise the Quaker involvement in railways could scarcely have flourished. Robert Ransome (1753-1830) is chiefly known for his agricultural machinery but, in partnership with Charles May (1801-1860), patented chairs and fastenings in rail laying. Thomas Clarke Worsdell (1788-1862) was entrusted with the first passenger coaches on the 1830 Liverpool & Manchester Railway. Thomas Edmondson (1792-1851) first devised the railway ticket while station master on the Newcastle & Carlisle Railway, and in 1841 set up in Manchester as an independent printer of railway tickets – a business continued until as late as 1960. George Bradshaw (1801-1853), an engraver and printer, brought out his first railway timetable in 1839. These are but a few of the many Quakers who were involved in the development of the railway system.

Panel D7

Botanists and Gardeners

The colonisation and exploration of the New World provided Friends with opportunities to develop botanical interests. Among them were zealous amateurs like Thomas Lawson (1630-1691), north country schoolmaster botanist, and professionals like John Bartram (1699-1777) of Pennsylvania, who was appointed the King's Botanist in America in 1765. Friends introducing new plants included Peter Collinson, FRS, (1693-1768), London mercer, and John Fothergill (1712-1780), eminent physician. John Coakley Lettsom (1744-1815), a medical colleague, helped to develop better ways of transporting seed and plants across the seas.

Captain Cook's voyage to the South Seas in *The Endeavour* included examination of the flowers and fruit met on the journey, when Sir Joseph Banks employed the Quaker Sydney Parkinson (c1745-1771) as an artist: he made nearly 1,000 botanical drawings in three years.

William Curtis (1746-1799) was in charge of the Chelsea Physic Garden for some years, and started *Curtis's Botanical Magazine* in 1787, with handcoloured plates. Curtis and his descendants ran a nursery, a trade which became particularly attractive to Friends. James Maddock the elder (c1715-1786) and his son, James (1793-1825), founded and developed Walworth Nursery. James Backhouse (1794-1869), Quaker minister to the convict settlements in Australia, returned to his brother and their nursery at York, which eventually occupied 100 acres. Sir Thomas Hanbury (1832-1907) established the famous garden at La Mortola, Liguria, Italy in 1867. Daniel Oliver (1830-1916), Professor of Botany in London, was Keeper of the Kew Herbarium 1864-1890.

The plants illustrated in this panel are a selection from the many associated with Quaker plant collectors. The quotation from Sarah Martha Baker, biochemist and lecturer at University College, London, serves as a reminder of the wide range of her interests from the ecology of seaweeds to the bread-making properties of alternatives to wheaten flour.

Panel D8

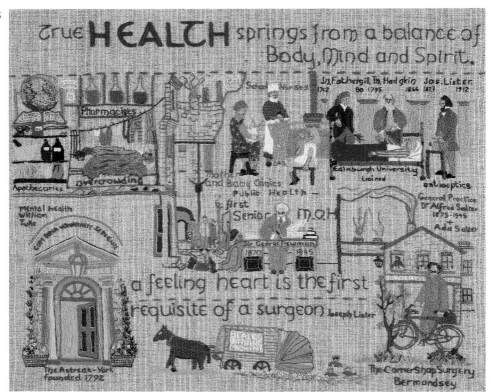

True **HEALTH** springs from a balance of Body, Mind and Spirit.

a feeling heart is the first requisite of a surgeon Joseph Lister

Quaker Doctors

Debarred until 1870 from Oxford and Cambridge Universities, Quaker medical men usually started as apprentices to apothecaries, some supplementing this experience by attending Leyden or Edinburgh (or, later on, University College, London). Quaker doctors relied on personal observation and mature reflection on the symptoms they saw, when it was more general for doctors to rely on preconceived ideas on the nature of illness and on dogmatically held systems of treatment. It is not surprising, then, that there was early emphasis on preventive and social medicine – John Fothergill put increasing stress on diet and regular habits of life, including fresh air and exercise; John Coakley Lettsom (1744-1815) opened the Aldersgate Dispensary and General Sea-bathing Infirmary, Margate, in 1796, "for the benefit of poor scrofulous children". Margate was also the resort where Benjamin Beale provided, in the 1770s, bathing machines with modesty-hoods.

Thomas Hodgkin (1798-1866) is best known for his 1832 paper "On some morbid appearances of the adsorbent glands and spleen", a discovery later to be known as Hodgkin's Disease. He was active in the establishment of the Aborigines Protection Society and a friend of Joseph Jackson Lister, father of Joseph Lister (1827-1912), the founder of antiseptic surgery. Alfred Salter campaigned for tree-lined streets throughout Bermondsey (which are still there); both he and George Newman (Chief Medical Officer of Health, 1919-35) were preoccupied with housing conditions and problems of infant mortality. And it was a layman of York, tea merchant William Tuke, who helped practically in the movement for the humane treatment of mental illness by promoting the foundation of The Retreat, York.

This panel recalls but a few names from the long succession of Quakers involved in medicine, from the pharmacists of the 17th and 18th centuries to such recent Friends as W. Russell Brain.

Panel D9

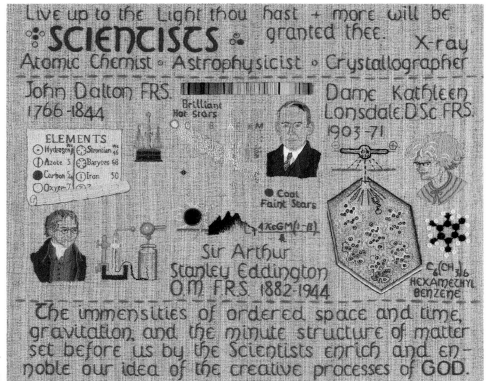

Quaker Scientists

"The pursuit of science springs from a striving which the mind is impelled to follow, and a questing that will not be suppressed...the striving born with our consciousness of an Inner Light proceeding from a greater power than ours" – Arthur S. Eddington.

John Dalton (1766-1844), who came of a Cumberland family of weavers, was appointed Professor of Mathematics and Natural Philosophy, Manchester, when 27 years old. He devised an atomic theory which led to the determination of the atomic weight of some gases, and the eventual compilation of the Table of Atomic Weights.

Arthur Stanley Eddington (1882-1944) had outstanding educational success in mathematics and physics. After five years at Greenwich Observatory, he was appointed Professor of Astronomy and Director of the Observatory at Cambridge University. He was the founder of modern theoretical astrophysics and, through his research at the 1919 eclipse of the sun, he was able to verify Einstein's Theory of Relativity.

Kathleen Lonsdale (1909-1971) graduated at 19 years, and embarked on research into crystal structures and the X-ray diffraction of crystals. She was Professor of Chemistry at University College, London, from 1949, and crystallography and associated medical problems occupied her professional life. She had become a Friend in 1935 and was tireless in her work for peace. She underwent an imprisonment in Holloway for refusing to register for firewatching (which she was doing voluntarily) and this aroused an interest in penal reform.

All three represented on this panel were Fellows of the Royal Society.

Panel D10

since the **17. INDUSTRIAL WELFARE** has developed as an expression of Quaker faith

Industrial Welfare

From early days, when the London (Quaker) Lead Company evolved, welfare of their workpeople has been seen as a Christian duty by Quaker employers, regarding all men and women equally as having "that of God" in them. There could be many examples from well-known Quaker firms of the past: Huntley & Palmer's, biscuit makers, is selected here, but perhaps the cocoa and chocolate firms are those synonymous with industrial welfare.

Richard and George Cadbury had a vision of their factory being in healthy and beautiful countryside, and Bournville was created. In 1846 an Irish Quaker, John Grubb Richardson, built his new linen mill at Bessbrook, with the intention of making a work-place to be good for the life of his employees; others had similar ideas. From 1879 Cadbury's, with their Bournville complex outside Birmingham, had a more comprehensive aim. Even at the earlier factory, free breakfasts were given to workers arriving at 6 a.m., and cotton uniforms for girls. At Bournville the welfare expanded to include medical care and recreation facilities. There were houses with gardens at modest rents, hostels, almshouses for the retired, pension plans and a savings scheme, smaller school classes and an adult education institute.

Rowntree's was another firm active in addressing the possibility of improving workers' lives. Joseph Rowntree, impressed by Bournville, founded in 1904 the model village of New Earswick and in the same year established the three trusts which enable his vision to continue.

Cherish the beauty + variety of his world

QUERY 19
Are you concerned that man's increasing power over nature should not be used irresponsibly but with reverence for life and with a sense of the splendour of God's continuing creation?

Query 19
Ecology

The world is a unit, all forms of life are interdependent, and yet, through greed in industrial nations and poverty in poor countries, plant species, insects and animals disappear daily. Dead lakes, ruined forests, air pollution and waste of resources are endemic in the present way of life. Deserts increase; seas are dustbins for human, industrial and nuclear refuse. Farmland suffers from soil erosion and loss of fertility through intensive cultivation, the use of heavy machinery and lack of organic matter. Soluble chemical fertilisers and pesticides poison rivers and underground reservoirs, thus entering the food chain to kill beneficial creatures, flowers and insects, and affect human beings.

A reverence for life is essential to Quaker witness, as expressed in this panel's Query. At the top the panel shows pollution to be prevented; smoke and noxious gases from industry and transport. Centrally, the need for industry is recognised by suggesting an advanced centre built on energy-saving principles, with reflective glass, giving a healthy working site and one designed to harmonise with a sensitively planned environment. Children embroidered the "free-range" ducks emerging from the lake, and recognised one endangered species by including a frog in the undergrowth. This "green and pleasant land" is completed with the distant farm worked by organic husbandry, hedges against soil erosion, and companion planting such as onions and carrots, marigolds and aromatic herbs, to deter pests.

We must be mindful that the planet which God has given us for a dwelling place, is given in stewardship.

Panel D12

Not yet designed

The Scott-Bader Commonwealth

It was in 1912 that Ernest Bader (1890-1982), son of a Swiss farmer, came to Britain, where he decided to settle. In 1920 he founded a company which became sole agent for a Swiss manufacturer of celluloid. He became a pioneer in the sale of nitrocellulose, which enabled a car to be painted in a matter of hours rather than days. The firm was first of all a trading concern, but about 1930 Ernest Bader turned to manufacture. In 1940 he moved his factory from Stratford, east London, to a manor house at Woollaston, near Wellingborough, Northamptonshire: there, with 44 acres of land, was plenty of room for factory buildings without destroying the essential character of house or gardens.

The range of goods steadily increased. The firm introduced the first styrenated polyester available in Europe and thus played a unique part in shaping the early history of the glass fibre reinforced plastics industry.

All this would have been achievement, but it is for the development of the Scott-Bader Commonwealth that Ernest Bader must be remembered. He was an industrial realist, but he had also from early years been a pacifist idealist and he and his wife had joined the Society of Friends in 1945. After looking at a number of options for the greater participation of all employees in the company, he created in 1951 the Commonwealth, giving it his own shares in the family company so that (other shareholders having done likewise) the Commonwealth now owns the company.

Membership of the Commonwealth is limited to employees of the company who are over 18 and have been with it at least a year, so that most employees are in fact members. This is fundamentally different from encouraging employees to become shareholders since, because all shares belong to the Commonwealth, all members of it are on an equality. As E.F. Schumacher noted in his *Small is beautiful* (1973), this transfer of ownership has changed the whole concept so fundamentally "that it would be better to think of such a transfer as effecting the extinction of private ownership rather than as the establishment of collective ownership".

Panel D13

GEORGE FOX at ULVERSTON
His experience of true healing

I looked at it in the love of God and the Lord's power sprang through me and through my hand. G.F. Journal

George Fox at Ulverston: Healing

George Fox was, in William Penn's words, "an original, being no Man's copy": a man of large physique, firm character, and an extremely powerful personality. Many found themselves pierced beyond bearing by his powerful eyes: "Do not pierce me so with thy eyes" cried one man in fear, "keep thy eyes off me". Fox had great powers of discernment which made him sensitive to the condition of his hearers, and sometimes gave him intimations of future happenings. He was both prophet and mystic: one who declared to his age the will and purpose of God, and who had received a personal experience of spiritual revelation.

There are some one hundred and fifty accounts of healings in which Fox was concerned, about half of which would appear to be cases of mental illness or possession. Thomas Ellwood's edition of the *Journal*, published in 1694 after Fox's death, removed many of the stranger stories, in case readers should confuse Quakerism with superstition.

The episode at Ulverston where Fox was first beaten unconscious and then struck so violently on the hand that it appeared useless, is a revealing one. "I looked at it (his hand) in the love of God, for I was in the love of God to them all that had persecuted me, and after a while the Lord's power sprang through me again, and through my hand and arm....". His motive in accepting persecution was to express a spirit of love through which other men might become gentle and loving, and so know God. "Whom God loves", wrote Fox, "He loves to the end; where the eternal unity is, there is all peace".

Panel E1

'a very phenomenon in the history of political economy' ~ Karl Marx

JOHN BELLERS 1654~1725

To the Lords + Commons in Parliament Assembled

proposals
1695 a colledge of industry
1697 education of children
1699, 1714 and 1723
   protection of poor and
no death penalty for fellons
1710 an European State and
Council of Christian persuasion
1712 ease of elections
1714 improvement of physick 1702 1714 Queen Anne

the poor without imployment are as rough diamonds their worth is unknown

John Bellers

John Bellers (1654-1725), a London Quaker cloth merchant, prospered and became a landed gentleman with wide interests, and a member of The Royal Society. After marriage he lived first in Chalfont St.Peter, then in Coln St.Alwyn, Gloucestershire. He was a member of Meeting for Sufferings and took considerable share in Quaker administration. He was twice imprisoned (1684,1685) for being at a Quaker meeting (described as a "Riotous Assembly"). He wrote a succession of papers – some addressed to Queen Anne, others in the form of petitions to Parliament – on unemployment, the death penalty, a central senate for Europe, a comprehensive health service, and care for refugees from religious persecution overseas. He believed that wealth should be usefully employed in creating jobs and prosperity, and that reform of the criminal was the first aim of punishment. Among his proposals were:

> Colleges of industry where the poor and unemployed would become independent of relief; Education for all children; Abolition of the death penalty for felony; Eradication of bribery and corruption from elections; Free health service for the poor; a system of medical education backed by research; a European state with a Parliament and a Council of representatives of religious groups to end disputes.

His writings were largely ignored, but were studied later by students of reform such as Robert Owen, Karl Marx and Joseph Rowntree. He died in 1725 a few years after he had written "...if a man shall not be heard in the age and country he lives in ....he may be more minded in other countries or succeeding generations".

Panel E2

The Quaker Trade of
BANKERING
Many Quaker Banks merged to form the core of well known Companies

Jonathan Backhouse balances the cash 1819

Honesty in business and the payment in full of debts justly incurred

Bankering

Quaker discipline has always insisted on probity – "Are you honest and truthful in word and deed? Do you maintain strict integrity in your business transactions...? Are you personally scrupulous and responsible in the use of money entrusted to you...?" Quakers were trusted in the stewardship of monies, and their banks grew numerous, most of them of regional importance before amalgamation. Backhouse & Company was one such bank, developed from the Backhouse family firm of linen manufacturers in Darlington.

In 1819 Lord Darlington resolved to "break" Backhouse's bank, in retaliation for Jonathan Backhouse having supported the building of a railway to Stockton-on-Tees to carry coal and won the day, instead of the canal his Lordship favoured. The Earl ordered his tenants to pay their rents with Backhouse's notes, intending to collect enough and present them for payment in gold when he had more than the bank could cover at a sudden demand. Jonathan Backhouse heard of this, and hastened to London to obtain a large amount of gold. Returning over Croft Bridge, a forewheel of his coach fell off! Rather than wait for repairs, he "balanced the cash" by piling it in the opposite corner of the coach, and returned to Darlington on three wheels! When Lord Darlington's Agent presented a large parcel of notes, they were promptly cashed. The bank accounts appear to confirm the story with an entry for 25th June 1819, "To Bank and Cash to London £32,000" and the later debit entry for £2.3.0. for a wheel.

CRIMINAL JUSTICE As a Quaker
I believe there is that of God in all people

though it's sometimes hard to find. Punishment ought to be a way of helping people to realise the hurt they are doing to this sense of worth in themselves + in others.
Harvey Gillman

Criminal
Justice

Very many early Quakers had personal experience of the appalling conditions in 17th century gaols. After that, few Quakers had any experience of prison life until they found themselves in gaol for conscience sake in the first world war. From the 1920s Friends began to question hitherto unquestioned assumptions. Quaker magistrates, members of the prison service, probation officers, prison visitors and Friends in general were increasingly asking, "What are we trying to do?"

A Penal Affairs Committee helps the Society of Friends to be well informed on both the spiritual and political planes, and to promote a more humane and non-punitive approach to offenders. One line of radical reform was published in *Six Quakers look at crime and punishment.* They note that criminals do not identify themselves with society, but consider themselves outside it; a court experience should bring an offender into the community rather than further separating him from it. "In all cases of offences against people, their lives and property, we should like to see the charge brought by the offended party". The police role would be detection and arrest, and crime prevention. In the community courts envisaged, it would be the court's duty to see that the complainant received satisfaction, by receiving restitution or reparation for the wrong done, not just seeing the offender suffer. The aims of such courts would involve facing the offender not only with his victim (at present the victim has no right to participate), but also "firmly and directly with the consequences of what he has done...of those consequences he was the cause, so...he should also be the cure".

The children's drawings in the lower section illustrate George Fox in Scarborough Castle being soaked with rain and waves; a young man doing community service; family visiting a prisoner, with prison officer carrying keys.

Panel E4

ELIZABETH FRY 1780 1845

Lord I believe - help thou my unbelief

By her inspiration devotion + charm she attracted public support for her concern to lighten the suffering + humiliation of prisoners

Elizabeth
Fry

Elizabeth Fry (1780-1845) was born into the Gurney family in Norwich, growing up in Earlham Hall on the outskirts of the city. Her childhood and youth, when she enjoyed music and dancing, was not that of "Plain" Friends: she and her sisters are depicted in the panel attempting to hold up the Norwich Mail. At seventeen she was profoundly influenced by the preaching of the American Quaker, William Savery, in Goats Lane Meeting House. At twenty she married Joseph Fry; she was the mother of eleven children, and for some years was submerged in domestic life. Although her charity had always embraced the immediate poor, her first visit to Newgate, instigated by Stephen Grellet(see Panel B5), was not until 1813. Amid the appalling conditions of filth, overcrowding and vicious living which she found there, she discovered in herself an extraordinary power over an audience. As a girl she had suffered greatly from nervous anxiety. Now this was channelled into the service of others, which she offered with complete confidence in the rightness of the work. Tall and well-built, dignified in the Quaker gown and bonnet, she used her outstandingly beautiful voice to great effect in Bible reading and prayers; above all, believing in the humanity of the prisoners, she treated them kindly but firmly, with a respect for them as individuals which the miserable women had never known.

It was one thing, however, to read the Bible to the prisoners, to appeal to their basic human dignity, to persuade them to co-operate in doing something for the children. It was another thing to appeal to rulers and governments or to try to modify popular opinion. In 1818, when she appeared before a House of Commons Committee, she was congratulated on her achievements. In 1832 the mood had changed and she was closely questioned as to "whether her views did not tend to the encouragement of crime rather than its prevention". In 1832 the treadmill was seen by the authorities as preferable to needlework.

Panel E5

1818-43 **ELIZABETH FRY** visited every ship taking women convicts-children to Botany Bay

106 ships, 12,000 souls

Women used to be taken to the docks in irons in open carts-this was ended-many people helped to improve shipboard conditions

School-sewing groups were started for those who wished

Each woman was given a bag of useful things

Elizabeth Fry and the Patchwork Quilts

In the 19th Century, among the thousands sentenced to be transported were many women, and in addition to her work in the prisons Elizabeth Fry did much to alleviate their conditions. She was able to persuade the authorities to introduce changes that made the journey more bearable, and she helped the women to organise themselves into groups for mutual help during the voyage. With the help of the British Society of Ladies, it was arranged that each woman would receive gifts, including one Bible, two aprons, one black cotton cap, one large hessian bag to keep her clothes in, one small bag containing one piece of tape, one ounce of pins, one hundred needles, nine balls of sewing cotton in different colours, twenty-four hanks of coloured thread, eight darning needles and one small bodkin; two stay laces, one thimble, one pair of scissors, one pair of spectacles when required, two pounds of patchwork pieces, two combs, knife and fork and a ball of string. The gifts had been chosen to be of great use to the woman, for among them was all the equipment needed to make a patchwork quilt. The quilting could occupy some of the long hours of the journey, and the quilt might be sold for a guinea when the boat called in at Rio de Janeiro, or when the woman reached Australia, where it could also be proof of her skill with the needle. The sum thus raised meant that she would not be destitute in the new country, and might have some way of earning a living.

Elizabeth Fry visited nearly every convict ship carrying women prisoners to the colonies from 1818 until her final illness in 1843. A total of 106 ships and 12,000 convicts came under her care. It was not until after her death that the force of public opinion led to the abolition of transportation, but at least some of the 12,000 had sailed with more hope for the future.

Panel E6

FIRST DAY SCHOOLS and the ADULT SCHOOLS MOVEMENT

—the ideas of religion - service - education and fellowship were held together

1847-1904. Forty Thousand Birmingham Early morning Students joined classes in the Institutes

Pioneers of the movement
Joseph Sturge
Samuel Fox
William White
Joseph Rowntree

Love not dogma, life not creeds

Adult Schools

In the late 18th Century, philanthropists like Robert Raikes began Sunday Schools, but a Friend, Joseph Lancaster, in 1798, began the successful British (Lancasterian) Schools, some of which opened for adults on First Day afternoons. The true roots of Friends' Adult Schools, however, can be traced to a Nottingham Methodist who founded a school for adults. This inspired a local Quaker, Samuel Fox, whose school was held from 7 to 9 a.m. on First Day. Years later, Joseph Sturge was impressed to learn of this First-day School, and in 1845 he opened an Adult School on Sunday evenings at the British School, Severn Street, Birmingham, and such schools multiplied. Instruction was provided by Friends, on the principle of fellowship among men, with the aim of teaching reading, particularly of the scriptures, and writing.

The Friends' First Day School Association was formed in 1847; William White, a Birmingham Quaker printer, was the movement's foremost advocate for the rest of the century. Many schools were built, often adjoining Quaker Meetings. For generations of Friends, teaching there was a "successful form of Christian endeavour", liberating "pent up energies in a sphere of fruitful service", in the words of John Wilhelm Rowntree. Adult Schools introduced other activities, e.g. libraries, sick clubs, and Joseph Rowntree started Adult Schools Cooperative Holidays in 1896.

In 1908 there were 496 Friends' Adult Schools with an average attendance of over 26,000. In view of the rapid growth of other Adult Schools, the work was merged in a wider body, later constituted as the National Adult School Union. Peak membership was in 1910, but declined as state education removed the original need. Some Adult Schools still exist, but Friends are not now corporately associated with them.

Panel E7

The Great Hunger

The failure of the potato crop in 1846 and 1847, as a result of potato blight, created a disastrous famine in Ireland. It was, for nearly three and a half million of the eight million population of Ireland, almost their only food as well as their chief means of obtaining the necessities of life. Friends set up a Relief Committee; the first practical aid was the opening of a soup kitchen in Dublin in January 1847. This became the model for others across the country. William Forster and other Friends surveyed the distress throughout the land, and organised local agents for the distribution of relief. The two Irish secretaries of the committee in Dublin took a major share in the work. Joseph Bewley, the original promoter of the relief, ruined his health and died in 1851. Some £200,000 in money, food and clothing was distributed by Quakers, much of it received after an appeal by the Society of Friends in London to Friends in North America. Food was sent by ship to the West coast, one of the worst-hit areas, where the companions of starvation – dysentry and fever – were rife. By 1849 almost two million Irish had died or emigrated.

In 1852 the Relief Committee published a major report on the famine which sought to identify the causes – the result of endemic unemployment which seemed "to have arisen from the state of the law and the practice respecting the occupation and ownership of land, encumbered estates and absenteeism". Friends established a Model Farm in County Galway, to introduce improved agricultural methods, but it was short-lived.

Panel E8

"COMRADE" MARY HUGHES
Mayfair 1860
Whitechapel 1941

DEW DROP INN 71

Once we have said
'Our Father' in the morning we can treat
no one as a stranger for the rest of the day

WHITECHAPEL WESTMINSTER

Mary
Hughes

Mary Hughes (1860-1941) devoted her life to the poor and downtrodden. For her the only way to do this was to identify completely with their poverty. Born in Mayfair in 1860, the daughter of a leading Christian Socialist who was a judge and author of *Tom Brown's Schooldays,* she lived for part of her life with relations who were Anglican clergymen. She saw the needs of the working poor in rural Berkshire and then the poverty in Whitechapel in the East End of London. The tragic loss of her sister and brother-in-law on the Titanic seems to have consolidated her resolve to be completely selfless.

In her youth she went to Quaker Meetings when staying with an aunt in Falmouth; the war made her a Quaker in 1918. In 1926 she bought an old public house in Whitechapel and named it The Dewdrop Inn for Education and Joy, making it a community advice centre with an ever open door for troubled people. She was on the Board of Guardians and was a Justice of the Peace but it was her unconventional and instinctive response to people that was important. A nearby Anglican priest said "She was always there".

In her seventies she was knocked down by a tram whilst leading a march of unemployed to the Houses of Parliament, and, before being taken to hospital she insisted on dictating and signing an acceptance of responsibility for the accident, exonerating the tram driver from all blame. A blue plaque is on her old home - "Mary Hughes, 1860-1941, Friend of all in need, lived and worked here, 1926-1941".

Panel E9

Unemployment

Friends' social witness leads not only to the relief of distress, but to attempting to remove the causes of social evils in any possible practical way. "Believing in the value of each person before God, Friends are profoundly concerned about the effects of unemployment on millions of people. We cannot accept that it is God's will that our society should be so ordered that some of its members, through no fault of their own, are denied the rights, privileges and opportunities for spiritual development..." *Meeting for Sufferings, 1987.*

In 1926 Emma Noble of Swindon attended the Quaker Yearly Meeting, where the session on unemployment impressed her with the conviction that there was something *she* must do. She came home, packed her bags, and set off for the Rhondda valley: she and her husband were to remain there for nearly twenty years. Friends sent clothing, boots, money and food. At Trealaw an Educational Centre, for both practical and cultural activities, was set up. Peter Scott's initiatives began work schemes at Brynmawr: a boot factory; pig and poultry farming; and a furniture factory which achieved renown under Paul Matt, who became craft organiser for the many unemployed social clubs. There were similar projects elsewhere, for example through the Friends' Allotments Committee, which distributed seed and garden implements at manageable prices (nearly 30,000 tons of seed potatoes and 267,000 spades and forks) apart from other help.

In the 1980s similar work is done by groups around the country; craft employment such as book-binding and basketry, and, often with other churches, making known any means available for providing resources and employment through local co-operation. All this work has been on a small scale - for only in small scale efforts do Friends find that personal relationships can be developed.

Panel E10

Friends'
Provident
Institution

In 1828 a young master at Ackworth School died and left his wife with an unborn child and no income, dependent solely on other Friends for support. He had been a popular master with a great influence on many of his pupils and our panel depicts her offering them comfort. There was a feeling of deep concern for the plight of the widow and her child, and Samuel Tuke and Joseph Rowntree proposed the formation of an institution which would provide "mutual benefit, relief and maintenance of members and their families".

Britain was becoming an industrial society at the beginning of the 19th century, and there was then no welfare state or social security to help those in trouble. A number of provident institutions were set up but, without enough understanding of the problems involved, they failed, causing even more hardship than they had tried to alleviate. Caring alone is not enough: good intentions must be backed up by sound business and commonsense. Friends in Yorkshire, led by the concern felt for one small family, produced a sound and prudent scheme, which resulted in 1832 in the establishment of the Friends' Provident Institution. It started its work in one room over a baker's shop in Bradford, with one fulltime member of staff. Its Head Office is now a large building in Dorking, and there are branch offices all over this country and overseas. Its name is now The Friends' Provident Life Office and its slogan is "Friends for Life". The provision in its constitution that at least five of the directors had to be Quakers was discontinued in 1983.

Panel E11

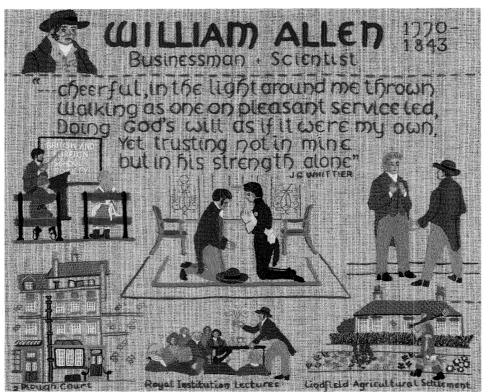

WILLIAM ALLEN 1770–1843
Businessman + Scientist

"... cheerful, in the light around me thrown,
Walking as one on pleasant service led,
Doing God's will as if it were my own,
Yet trusting not in mine,
but in his strength alone"
                                    J G WHITTIER

2 Plough Court   Royal Institution Lectures   Lindfield Agricultural Settlement

William Allen

William Allen (1770-1843) began by working for a Quaker pharmacist at Plough Court, London. He took over in 1795, developing laboratories and a manufactory, which was to become Allen & Hanbury Ltd. An inveterate experimenter, he was always seeking to develop his scientific knowledge. He lectured at Guy's Hospital until middle life and at the Royal Institution by invitation of Sir Humphrey Davy; he was elected Fellow of The Royal Society.

"Quakerism is essentially a religion of life, an attempt to practise the presence of God, to express the truth of it in practical living" (Rufus Jones), and that was how William Allen lived.

One life-long preoccupation was the British & Foreign Schools Society based on the ideas of Joseph Lancaster, Quaker educationalist. On his many travels William Allen sought to promote these ideas for educating the poor, and for prison reform, seeking the support of royalty and church leaders everywhere. Czar Alexander I had shown an interest in Quakerism when in London in 1814, and had met William Allen. On meeting again in Russia, they had a period of silent worship after discussions.

William Allen and Peter Bedford were close friends, always conscious of the poverty of many, active in alleviating the lot of the downtrodden with suitable help, a concern still recognised by the Bedford Institute Association in London's East End. In his later years, appalled at the ignorance and poverty of land labourers in Sussex, William Allen worked towards creating changes in a village, Lindfield, with a school of industry, library and allotments.

Panel E12

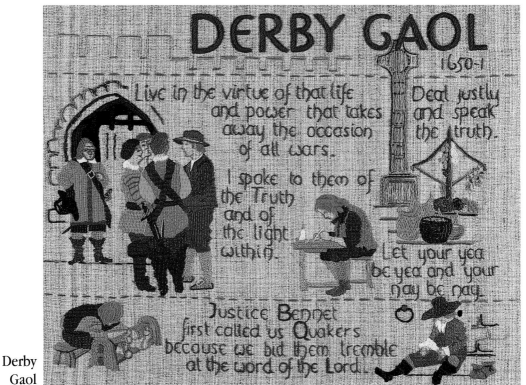

Derby Gaol

In the course of his travels in the east Midlands George Fox reached Derby in October 1650, speaking to the congregation in the steeplehouse of "the day of the Lord and the light within them". He was charged and imprisoned for blasphemy under the recently-passed Act. Towards the end of six months he was offered a captaincy in the Commonwealth army but responded in the words in the top centre of the panel. Not knowing that his "yea was yea and nay nay" they thought this an exchange of politenesses, and when they found him firm, he was hustled away into a dungeon "amongst thirty felons in a lousy stinking low place in the ground, without any bed". It was not until October 1651, after nearly a year in prison, that he was released.

Peace is dependent on just dealing. Fox had already appealed to merchants to deal justly and he would continue these appeals. The panel depicts a market cross and some of the merchandise. It was during this period, as Fox recalled, that Justice Bennet "first called us Quakers because we bid them tremble at the word of God". Early Friends referred to themselves as "Children of Light" or "Friends of Truth"; the description "Religious Society of Friends" began to be used in the late 18th Century.

WILLIAM PENN + WILLIAM MEADE
were tried for preaching to an unlawful assembly

The jury refused to give a verdict against them although fined + locked up without food. Their stand established the right of Juries to give their verdict according to their convictions. 1670

The Trial of
William Penn
and
William Meade

The second Conventicle Act (see Panel C3) came into force on 10 May 1670, its policy to ruin with heavy fines rather than imprison offenders. The Act was a signal for renewed attacks on all dissenters. On 14 August 1670 William Penn (son of the Admiral), William Meade (a prosperous linen draper), and their fellow Quakers found their meeting house in White Hart Court, Gracechurch Street, London, locked against them. They therefore proceeded to hold their meeting in the street. Penn and Meade were arrested, the indictment for a riot stating that Penn preached "in Contempt of ...the King, and of his Law, to the great disturbance of his Peace, to the great Terror and Disturbance of many of his Liege People and Subjects". The trial was before ten justices from 1 to 5 September, but no witnesses were able to testify to what Penn had said and, after a vigorous defence by Penn frequently interrupted by the bench, the jury brought in a verdict of "Guilty of speaking in Gracious-street" – which was, of course, no offence. The recorder who, with the mayor, had been the most menacing of the justices declared that the jury should not be dismissed till they brought in a verdict the court would accept and that they should be "lockt up without Meat, Drink, Fire and Tobacco". Penn after observing that "We did not make the Tumult, but they that interrupted us", turned to the jury with: "You are Englishmen; mind your Privilege; give not away your Right".

Despite the bench's threats the jury continued to return the same verdict until, a positive verdict being demanded, they returned "Not guilty", for which they were fined and imprisoned for refusal to pay the fines. One of the jurors, Edward Bushel, brought an action for unjust imprisonment against the mayor and recorder: for a year the case hung in doubt, judgement finally being given by Chief Justice Vaughan, no friend to nonconformity, in a speech of two or three hours' duration, establishing the firm principle of the right of juries to bring in a free verdict for which they could not be punished. It was, wrote Penn, "the fairest flower that now grows in the garden of the Englishman's liberties".

Panel F2

British Quakers protest to parliament against
THE SLAVE TRADE in 1783

God hath made of one blood all nations of men for to dwell upon the face of the earth. ACTS.17. VERSE 26

YEARLY MEETING — GRACECHURCH STREET

Slavery continues and is a reproach to humanity.

The Slave Trade

As early as 1657 Fox had seen the danger of the master-slave relationship, and his 1671 visit to America led him to increased concern for the welfare of slaves. The Irish Quaker, William Edmundson, wrote in 1676 that "Perpetual slavery is an aggravation and oppression upon the mind". It was but gradually that Quakers came to the conviction that slave-owning was contrary to the belief that "God hath made of all nations one blood".

In 1772 John Woolman (see Panel A6) was at the Yearly Meeting in London: its epistle expressed the hope that the slave trade might be "utterly abolished". American Quakers now made strenuous efforts to get Friends in Britain to give political aid to achieving this. The American War of Independence (1775-82) meant that the political atmosphere was unpropitious but in 1783 the Yearly Meeting was ready to act, fully recognising that "we must expect to meet with the greatest opposition of interested parties".

The panel is based on the oil painting "Gracechurch Street Meeting about 1770". Women Friends met in a separate meeting for business and the Men's Yearly Meeting on 16 June sent a petition to Parliament signed by 273 Friends, urging that participation in the slave trade be forbidden absolutely. It was read aloud in the House of Commons the next day. This was the beginning of a vigorous campaign. In 1787 the Quaker committee was replaced by a national one, and the leadership of the movement was taken over by evangelical Anglicans, notably Wilberforce, Clarkson and Elizabeth Fry's brother-in-law, Fowell Buxton. Friends continued as ardent supporters of the campaign culminating in the 1807 Act which abolished the British slave trade, and the Emancipation Act 1833 which abolished slavery in the British dominions. This was, however, far from being the end of the fight against slavery in the world.

Panel F3

DANIEL WHEELER was engaged in 1818 by Czar Alexander I to clear + drain 105,700 acres of the St. Petersburg marshes.

God's love enableth me to call every country my country and every man my brother.

In later life he requested a ship that he might sail the South Seas to present the Quaker message.

Daniel Wheeler

Daniel Wheeler (1771-1840) was born in London, orphaned young and went to sea. After serving in both the British army and navy, he resigned his commission and became a successful seed merchant and farmer. In 1799 he joined the Society of Friends in Sheffield, becoming a recorded Minister.

In 1817 Czar Alexander I of Russia asked English Quakers to find him a Friend to supervise the agricultural experiments he was planning at St.Petersburg. Daniel Wheeler agreed to go, and with his wife, Jane, and their family, sailed for Russia in 1818. He was joined by the young George Edmondson (1798-1863), brother of Thomas, the inventor of the railway ticket (see Panel D7). In the course of fourteen years the vast acreage of marsh south of the city was cleared and valuable new methods of farming were introduced. The small company kept up Quaker meetings for worship, and it was in reflecting on one of these that he wrote in his journal the words inscribed on the panel, which also recalls the new fertile land near to the Russian capital.

In 1833, supported by Friends of his own meeting and by Meeting for Sufferings, which supplied a ship, the *Henry Freeling*, he set sail with his son, Charles, for Hobart where they met with James Backhouse and George Washington Walker (see Panel F20). They visited convict settlements and isolated Friends, continuing their journey to Tahiti, Hawaii and other Pacific Islands. Daniel Wheeler's purpose was not to make converts to Quakerism but to preach the Gospel and to reach that of God in everyone, whether convict, settler or native king. He regretted and tried to prevent the exploitation of natives, and the promotion of drink by sailors and traders.

The dolphins shown on the panel record the occasion of a severe storm when, by surrounding the *Henry Freeling* they broke the force of the waves on the threatened ship, and so saved it from disaster.

After two journeys to America, Daniel Wheeler died in New York in 1840.

Panel F4

Friends visit the Czar, 1854

In December 1853 there was a war fever in Britain, fanned by an anti-Russian press. Joseph Sturge (1793-1859) a Birmingham corn merchant, began to wonder whether any good might be effected by a Quaker delegation to the Czar Nicholas I of Russia. He brought his concern to Meeting for Sufferings on 6 January 1854, an address to the Czar was prepared and it was agreed that Joseph Sturge should go to St. Petersburg with Robert Charleton (1809-1872) a Bristol pin manufacturer, and Henry Pease (1807-1881), of Darlington, son of Edward Pease, "father of railways".

They left London on Friday, 20 January, at 8 am, and arrived in St.Petersburg on Thursday, 2 February, at 7 pm. They travelled by train to Königsberg, although they had to cross the River Vistula on the ice in a horse-drawn 'bus. They then travelled by coach to Riga and there, because the snow was too deep, they changed the wheels of their coach for sledge runners. For some of the journey they needed seven horses to pull them through the snow drifts. They calculated that they had used over 200 horses at a penny-half-penny per horse per mile.

They were well received by the Czar and in the capital in general, but this cordial atmosphere was suddenly changed because, as we now know (but they did not), diplomatic relations had been suspended by the British Foreign Office. They returned to meet the opprobrium of the British press. They had gone in no sense of foolish optimism, but from a conviction that this was a religious duty, and the longterm effects of personal relationships can never be measured.

Their return journey was completed in nine days.

RELIEF WORK - BRITAIN "Our life is helping one another up with a tender hand"

Peterloo Massacre 1819 Cotton Workers ridden down by militia at a meeting for Parliamentary Reform are given refuge in the Friends Meeting House Manchester

Mount St Shelter

Relief Work: British Isles

On August 16 1819 a large demonstration for Parliamentary reform at St. Peter's Field, Manchester, ended as the Peterloo Massacre, when the Manchester Yeomanry Cavalry put down the protest at a cost of eleven killed and four hundred injured. The Friends Meeting House in South Street, adjacent to the field, is described as having "served as a refuge for fugitive men, women and children, swept before the Yeomanry...For many months afterwards its floor was stained with the marks of human blood".

The new 1830 Meeting House faced Mount Street and the panel, under the roof line of the basement, recalls some of the work undertaken there. The left recalls the work of the Manchester and District Refugee Committee, set up by local Quakers in 1938 with 2,250 German and Austrian refugees on its case books. A special feature for raising funds was the annual exhibition/sale of refugee handicrafts. This was part of a nationwide effort by many refugee organisations during the 1930s, among them the Germany Emergency Committee set up by Quakers in 1933; its secretary , Bertha L. Bracey, deserves continuing remembrance for her fearless and untiring work for the refugees.

The child in the centre is a reminder that, on the outbreak of war in 1939,the Overseers at Manchester and Liverpool cooperated to sponsor a scheme for the evacuation of Friends' children from 3 to 12 years old to Yealand Manor in North Lancashire, a school that became an educational experiment.

On the right we are transported from Manchester to London, where Friends as well as many others were active during the Blitz of the Second World War in arranging for the evacuation of those not covered by official schemes, notably elderly people and mothers and children. The welfare of those in shelters is one of the themes of Panel F8.

Panel F6

In the **RELIEF of SUFFERING**
we maintain the principle of impartial giving to all,
of whichever nation, race, creed or class are in need

1947 FSC·AFSC
shared the
Nobel Peace Prize

Quaker teams assess
situations + channel
aid through local
committees

Châlons Maternité
1914-7 3,789 patients

Caring for Displaced
Persons 1945-7

Training Centres 1938-45
Mount Waltham, Hampstead,·Spiceland, Devonshire
Relief workers need self-discipline·basic skills as well as
loving concern, building bridges of reconciliation

**Relief of
Suffering**

From the Napoleonic Wars onwards, Quakers have sought to give expression to their peace testimony by helping, in some small measure, to bind up some of the wounds of war. During and after both world wars Quaker teams (including many likeminded folk as well as Friends) were active, concentrating always on smallish schemes which would help to fill gaps that large-scale relief could not cope with. Teams have worked in France, Netherlands, Germany, Austria, Poland, Russia and Greece.

The red and black eight-pointed star was first used in 1870 when Quakers also made clear in their posters that their relief was offered to non-combatants whether French or German who had suffered in the war. This policy of impartiality has been conscientiously maintained, though all too frequently misunderstood.

In 1914 Friends set up a maternity hospital at Chalons-sur-Marne. Established in inadequate buildings, subjected to shelling and bombing, it included a children's clinic and creche, and in five years there were nearly 1,000 births with the death of only one mother.   In 1919 it was handed over to a French committee and new buildings were opened in 1922.

To the right we are reminded of the displaced persons – Poles, Balts, Ukranians, Yugoslavs and others brought in to work compulsorily in German factories, and who at the end of the war could not or would not return home. In 1948 there were still 212,000 in the British zone in need of immediate welfare as well as the solution of an uncertain future.

In 1947 British and American Friends Service Councils were joint recipients of the Nobel Peace Prize. The presentation address included the words, "For it is not the extent of their work or its practical form which is more important in assessing the services rendered by the Quakers....It is rather the spirit which animates their work."

Panel F7

Friends
Ambulance
Unit

In the world wars of this century, the Society of Friends has maintained its testimony against all war, whilst individual members have been free to follow their own conscience. For many, conscientious objection alone was not the complete answer; a more positive action of healing the wounds was required.

In 1914 a group of Quakers set up a Friends Ambulance Unit which over the next five years had 1700 members, far from all of them Friends. It worked in civilian and military hospitals in France, with French convoys, in hospital ships and on ambulance trains. There was also a Home Section working in hospitals in this country. The FAU was revived in 1939 and on 7 September 1940, with the onset of air raids, those members working in east London hospitals found themselves plunged into civilian relief work, which ultimately occupied 200 members of the Unit. The panel also commemorates FAU team work overseas – in Syria and Ethiopia, India and China, Greece and north-west Europe. In particular it recalls the work of the China convoy. In 1942, with eleven trucks lost in Burma, the age of petrol and plentiful spare parts was over, and that of the charcoal burner had arrived. Lying under a lorry, attempting the repairs, was "more the rule than the exception in West China".

Panel F8

SERVICE is love in action

The Visitors Centre Maze Prison

...listen to people on both sides and maybe help them to listen to one another

Quaker Cottage Belfast

Reconciliation

The Quaker realisation that the Inward Light of God is given in measure to all men underlines the significance of the brotherhood of men. When conflicts and disputes occur between people or groups of people, Friends know that the way of reconciliation offers the best solution for bringing the parties to dialogue and friendship.

Immediate relief implies long-term responsibility. A testimony against all war implies a testimony for peace-making and reconciliation. Quakers in Northern Ireland committed themselves to two small but demanding ventures in which personal relationships could be built up. At the Maze Prison a canteen and children's playroom for visiting families provides the background for listening to often bewildered people; and at Quaker Cottage children from both sides of the torn community are able to enjoy holidays together. They have a mini-bus and support many other schemes, e.g. family holidays in caravans for people in special need; the Belfast Lunch Club for the elderly; mothers and young children's groups: and not least, Quaker House in Belfast, where Friends attempt to promote understanding among the people of Northern Ireland at all levels.

Friends, in their work in reconciliation, would re-echo the words of Rufus M. Jones (1863-1948), an American Quaker and philosopher: "I pin my hopes to quiet processes and small circles in which vital and transforming events take place".

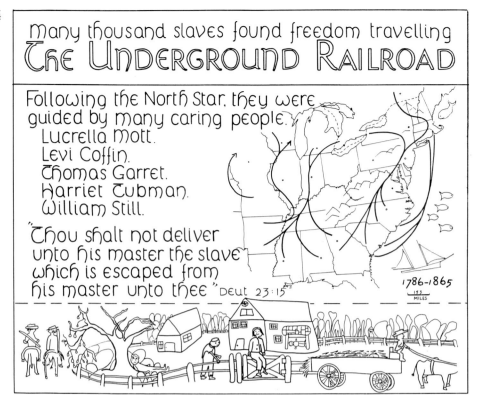

Many thousand slaves found freedom travelling
The Underground Railroad

Following the North Star, they were guided by many caring people.
Lucretia Mott.
Levi Coffin.
Thomas Garret.
Harriet Tubman.
William Still.

"Thou shalt not deliver unto his master the slave which is escaped from his master unto thee" Deut 23:15

1786-1865
153 MILES

The Underground Railroad

In 1786 George Washington mentioned a group of Philadelphian Quakers who had tried to help an escaping negro slave, and a Fugitive Slave Law of 1793 shows that the authorities felt the need to suppress similar activities.

After 1807, when the slave trade was abolished in Britain and her colonies, and even more after the Emancipation Act of 1833, Canada became a safe haven for escaping slaves. It was towards Canada therefore that the Underground Railroad worked its development of "stations" and "lines", by which single fugitives and groups were taken or directed from one "safe house" to another.

The panel shows a map of the main lines of the railroad; there must have been many branch lines. Conductors had to be brave, calm and resourceful, discreet and trustworthy, and many adventures are told of hairbreadth escapes and of the outwitting of the pursuers. Many Quakers were deeply involved and some were among the leaders. Of the names on the panel, Levi Coffin and Thomas Garrett were Quakers; Harriet Tubman and William Still were negroes, the latter free-born and secretary of an organising committee, the former herself an escaped slave, who made courageous journeys to collect fugitives. These two represent the numbers of those not members of the Society with whom Friends worked.

Panel F10

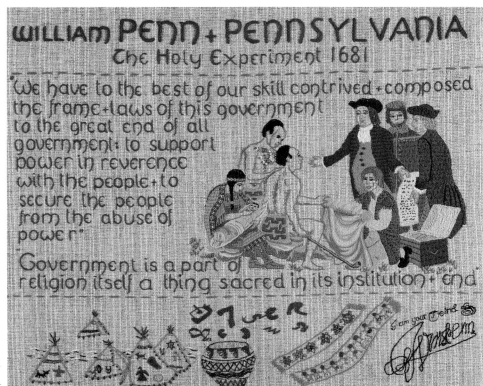

WILLIAM **PENN + PENNSYLVANIA**
The Holy Experiment 1681

"We have to the best of our skill contrived + composed the frame + laws of this government to the great end of all government: to support power in reverence with the people + to secure the people from the abuse of power"

"Government is a part of religion itself a thing sacred in its institution + end"

Penn and Pennsylvania

From 1675 Friends began to emigrate to America in larger numbers. Puritan New England in 1660 had been inhospitable to the point of hanging three Quakers. In Rhode Island there had been toleration. The Jerseys were the earliest field of real enterprise. The 1681 grant from the Crown of the land Charles II named Pennsylvania (in repayment of a debt he owed Penn's father) led to an experiment in Quaker government which was to last, at times uneasily, for seventy years.

Penn envisaged his State as following Quaker principles of democracy, religious toleration, peaceful institutions, and under God's guidance, a Holy Experiment. The State's capital was named Philadelphia, City of Brotherly Love. The Charter of Privileges for Pennsylvania was an inspirational element for the Constitution of the United States.

In a series of treaties based on mutual trust, Penn established good relations with the Leni-Lenape Indians. Benjamin West (1738-1820) depicted "the Great Treaty" under an elm tree at Shackamaxon: this painting, well-known from engravings, must be regarded as a work of historical imagination, perhaps representing a number of separate occasions. The panel shows the gifts presented by the Quakers to the Indians and, towards the right at the foot, a wampum belt as the Indian record of a treaty. At the far right is Penn's signature, and on the left the signatures of nine Indian chiefs, all copied from original documents. And it was Voltaire who remarked that Penn's treaty with the Indians was the only treaty never sworn to and never broken.

Penn returned to England in 1684 but was briefly in Pennsylvania again from 1699 to 1701. His last years were spent at Ruscombe, near Twyford, Berks, and he is buried in the Friends Burial Ground at Jordans, Bucks.

Panel F11

LIVE Bring the whole of your daily life under the ordering of the spirit of Christ.

ADVENTUROUSLY

Nantucket whalers came to Milford Haven-1792

"When the war began we declared against taking any part of it..."

Gwyn ei byd yr oes a'u clyw,
Blessed is the generation that hears them.
Dangnefeddwyr, plant i Dduw,
The peacemakers, the children of God.

Waldo Williams 1904-71

America and
Milford Haven
Meeting

Edward Starbuck and his brother Nathaniel migrated to Nantucket Island, off the coast of Massachusetts, in 1659, along with some twenty other families. They developed a whaling industry, hunting the sperm whale as far as the Falklands. With the outbreak of the American War of Independence in 1775, the five thousand Quakers on the island refused to support either side, and their trade suffered badly. Tariffs were applied by Britain on American goods, which ruined the local whaling industry. A move to Nova Scotia brought them within a Colony again, but success was not assured.

The whalers therefore sought a base in Europe and some settled at Dunkirk in the 1780s, only to find fresh difficulties following the outbreak of the French Revolution. In 1792 some fifteen families landed at Milford Haven and a new town took shape under a Nova Scotian architect, typically North American – a market place and three main roads parallel to the shore, lanes crossing at right-angles. Whaling and shipbuilding developed for a while, and the hunting grounds were extended to Australian waters. At first Friends held Meetings for Worship at Haverfordwest; their own Meeting House was built in 1811. The whale-oil trade at Milford did not, however, succeed, and some of the younger generation eventually returned to America. No descendents of the immigrants now remain, but the Nantucket settlers are remembered by the plain gravestones in the Meeting House burial ground marked simply with their initials. The Meeting House is, however, now again well used.

The panel also commemorates Waldo Williams (1904-1971), a member of Milford Haven meeting, renowned Welsh poet and conscientious objector, who was imprisoned on two occasions for withholding tax in protest against the Korean war. He was deeply concerned for the improvement of living conditions in rural Wales and for the restoration to legal status of the Welsh language.

Panel F12

FIDELITY to the TRUTH led hundreds of QUAKERS from persecution in the DOLGELLAU area to the NEW WORLD in the SEVENTEENTH century

Cader Idris

Brynmawr

Owen Lewis Tyddyn y garreg d.1686

Pennsylvania

Quakers in Dolgellau

In the seventeenth century there had been a flourishing Yearly Meeting for Wales: by the early nineteenth century it was discontinued and there were but a few scattered meetings. There had been widespread emigration, particularly to Pennsylvania where the "Welsh tract" still bears reminders in Merion, Gwynedd, Bryn Mawr, Haverford and Radnor. The emigration, initially on account of persecution, continued into the 18th century as Quakers and others in an impoverished land sought better opportunities in the New World.   Some 4000-5000 Friends emigrated from Wales to America and it is perhaps no wonder that the Welsh Yearly Meeting lamented "runnings off to Pennsylvania".

The centre of the panel shows Tyddyn-y-garreg (The house by the rock), the home of the Owen family. Inside can still be seen the panelled room used for Friends' meetings before the Meeting House was built, and nearby is a plot of land given by Owen Lewis as a burial place in 1665. One of the regular worshippers here was Dorti Owen (1751-1793), who was an intrepid and valiant Friend, on occasions walking all the way to London and back to attend Yearly Meeting. It was due to her effort that the Meeting House was built nearby. Completed in 1792, it was retained by Friends for over fifty years. As their numbers declined, the building was eventually sold to the Welsh Independents, and renamed Capel Tabor.

The man on the left of the panel is Rowland Ellis (1650-1731) who lived at Brynmawr (not to be confused with the Brynmawr in Panel E10). In 1676 he and others were tried at Bala for not attending church and refusal to take the oath. Judge Walcott threatened them with hanging, but the sentence was remitted when they declared allegiance to the King and abhorrence of Popery. He was among the many who emigrated to Pennsylvania where he became Representative in the Assembly. The famous women's college, Bryn Mawr, near Philadelphia, stands on part of the estate he owned.

Panel F13

Quakerism in New Zealand/ Aotearoa

Aotearoa is the original name for New Zealand, meaning "Land of the long white cloud". In 1841 two Quakers, Thomas and Jane Mason, emigrated to New Zealand and settled in the Hutt Valley, buying their land from the Maoris. A disagreement with the Maoris led to 3,000 sheep being taken from "Quaker Mason", as he was generally known. The dispute was resolved through dialogue, and the Maoris respected the Masons for their courage and integrity. The patterned border (as shown at top right of the panel) is a Maori design, its wording "Tutu ana puaha" referring to oratory stirring up the listeners.

Friends are widely scattered in New Zealand, and their Summer Gathering each year provides opportunity for harmonious living together amid natural beauty with resulting refreshment for body and spirit. In the background is Frlends Settlement or Quaker Acres, the only residential Quaker community, built on land originally part of Friends School (1920-1969) in Wanganui. The tree on the left is the pohutukawa, which flowers at Christmas, with flax and a kiwi at the base, and the tui (the parson bird) eating honey from the flax flowers. The central tree is a kowhai. Two fantails hover over the group: they are usually to be seen wherever people gather together.

The flowers behind bars symbolise those taken each week by Auckland Friends from their Meeting to prisoners in Mount Eden jail. This custom began in the 1914-18 war, and has continued ever since. Each Christmas every prisoner receives a gift of flowers.

Panel F14

Workcamps

Quaker Workcamps owe much to Pierre Ceresole (1879-1973), Swiss Friend and founder of International Voluntary Service. "It is", he said, "ordinary life which is our essential and constant communion with God." Practical activities by Young Friends and others, such as those to alleviate the evils of unemployment in the 1930s, were following similar leadings and involving young people from all walks of life. Jack Hoyland (1887-1957), Woodbrooke lecturer and one-time mission worker in India, was a stalwart of the workcamps movement. Leaders are trained; workers are of varying ages, though often students.

The heart of a workcamp is in working together, often with those of different races, on a project in the value of which all believe, and with faith in a common humanity which allows identification with the needs of others. Typical recent projects have been – agricultural work in East Europe, the Ukraine and Turkey; building in Austria; building in the Pyrenees at a community visited by French city school children; renovating tools for use in Nicaragua; working in Belfast's Quaker Cottage (see Panel F9), and at Coleraine on the Peace People's Farm conservation centre; playgroups and holidays for children with and without physical and mental disabilities, and holidays for mentally handicapped adults; redecoration at a Buddhist monastery in England, while joining in discussion and meditation; work in a centre for mixed race families. A few camps are for women only, working in women's refuges.

Traditionally, work camps have been manual, even if not restricted to pick and shovel. Over the years, as these instances show and the foot of the panel illustrates, the emphasis has changed: this is reflected by their recent description as international social projects - more accurate though much less poetic.

Panel F15

TRUE PEACE cannot be dictated, it can only be built in co-operation between all peoples. Yearly Meeting 1943

Quaker United Nations Offices. Geneva, New York. Quaker Council for European Affairs. Brussels.

School of Peace Studies University of Bradford established 1972.

Every step to diminish fear is a step towards peace.

Co-operation is better than conflict.

Peace Embassies

Carl Heath (1869-1950), Secretary of the National Peace Council, was one of the speakers at a conference at Skipton at Easter 1917, organised by Yorkshire Friends. He had joined Friends the previous year and, commending the Quaker message as being "not of words but of life", pleaded for "the planting of a Quaker embassy in every European capital".

This vision was translated into the establishment of "Quaker centres" – Berlin, Paris, Geneva and (later) Delhi, to name a few. Some were shortlived, others have continued over the years. Their purpose has been less to do than to be; their hope has been that people of diverse faiths, races and cultures may discover for themselves the common ground underlying their diversity.

During the second world war a London Centre was opened and, following the establishment of the United Nations, Quakers worldwide received recognition as a non-governmental agency, leading to the opening of Quaker House, New York, and the Quaker United Nations Programme. During the postwar years British Friends organised a series of seminars for diplomats in the belief that, as they met one another in more informal surroundings, different and deeper relationships would be built up to the increase of mutual confidence. As the European Economic Community developed, the setting up of a Quaker Council for European Affairs and the opening of a Brussels Centre was a natural consequence.

It was in 1970 that the idea of a University Department of Peace Studies was propounded, leading the way to the establishment of such a department at the University of Bradford, founded jointly by the University and British Friends. In 1973 the Quaker Adam Curle was appointed to the chair, bringing to the task a wide knowledge of educational and social development in Africa, Asia and Central and South America, and the following year the doors were opened to students. The building of the institutions of peace needs disciplined thinking and informed study.

Panel F16

QUAKER VIGILS FOR PEACE
Trafalgar Square 1980

PEACE
BEGINS IN THE
HEARTS OF THE PEOPLE

We utterly deny all outward war + strife + fightings with outward weapons, for any end whatever... This is our testimony to the whole world

Vigils for Peace

Friends have begun to use the term "vigil" for a corporate silent witness. The panel depicts the witness in Trafalgar Square during Yearly Meeting 1980. A thousand Friends walked, two by two, in an exceedingly long crocodile, in groups of forty, badged and bannered, fore and aft. Such was the almost military precision of the organisation that, as six o'clock struck from St.Martin in the Fields, the last group reached the Square and the supporting group of saffron-robed Buddhists graciously ceased their drumming, as essential to their witness in the streets of London as silence is to the Quakers.

At Yearly Meeting at the University of Warwick in 1982 there was an ecumenical witness for peace in Coventry, when 2,000 Friends and others formed two groups, one holding their vigil in the ruins of the old cathedral, whilst others stood silently in the shopping precinct. All came together to fill the new Cathedral for an act of worship, where the Leaveners (see Panel C11) led the large congregation in singing Jan Struther's All-Day hymn, "Lord of all hopefulness, Lord of all joy".

The ecumenical element in public witness, whether silent or programmed, has been increasingly evident, as shown in many towns throughout the country during the Gulf War.

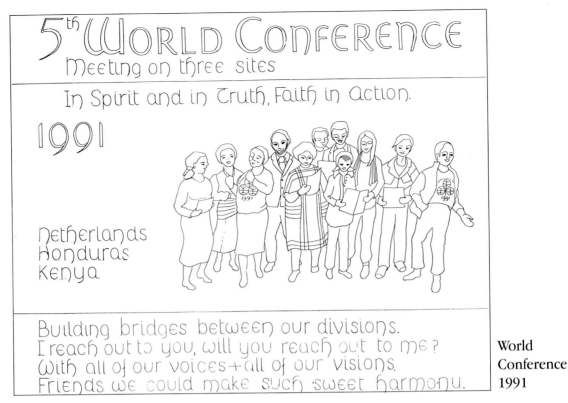

5th WORLD CONFERENCE
Meeting on three sites

In Spirit and in Truth, Faith in Action.

1991

Netherlands
Honduras
Kenya

Building bridges between our divisions.
I reach out to you, will you reach out to me?
With all of our voices + all of our visions,
Friends we could make such sweet harmony.

World
Conference
1991

In 1677 George Fox, William Penn and Robert Barclay visited the Netherlands in order to organise a yearly meeting for the continent of Europe. The Friends' meetings in other parts of the continent did not survive very long, but the concept of an organisation stretching beyond a single country or region was one to which Quakers would return.

At the beginning of the 19th Century there were six yearly meetings in North America: by the end of the century there were 27. Missionary activity by British and American Friends led to the establishment from the later 19th century of yearly meetings in various parts of Asia, Africa and South America while emigration from Britain led to the formation of yearly meetings for Australia, New Zealand and Central and Southern Africa.

Towards the end of the first world war, concern for re-expression of Friends' peace testimony led to the All Friends Conference (London, 1920). Subsequent World Conferences were held at Swarthmore College, Pennsylvania (1937), Oxford (1952) and Guilford College, North Carolina (1967). The fifth World Conference was held in 1991 in three locations – in June at Elspeet, Netherlands, in July in Honduras, and in August in Kenya – each having world and not merely regional representation.

From 1931, with many new Quaker meetings on the continent of Europe, a series of annual conferences developed, now firmly established as the European & Near East Section of Friends World Committee for Consultation.

In 1920 Quakerism was still substantially Anglo-American. This is no longer true. At the 1920 Conference there was an attendance of 936 of whom 890 were from Britain, Ireland and North America and 46 from the rest of the world. In 1991 there was an attendance of 1027 of whom 490 were from Britain, Ireland and North America and 537 from the rest of the world.

Panel F18

Quakerism in South Africa

Though there were a few Dutch Quakers in South Africa in the early 18th Century, it was a short-lived group. It was the later 19th Century before emigration brought British Friends to South Africa and they were very few in a vast land.

From 1903 a Friends Meeting was held in Cape Town, a Monthly Meeting of London Yearly Meeting. South Africa General Meeting was first held in 1918, and in 1946 Southern Africa Yearly Meeting was established.

During the Anglo-Boer War (1899-1902) Quakers engaged in relief work in the camps to which Boer women and children had been moved, as well as attempting, by listening to people on both sides, to increase mutual understanding. Friends learned that among all the destruction and looting of farms, soldiers had taken as souvenirs many large, heavily bound, family Bibles, often containing a wealth of family records. Many of these Bibles were located and returned to the original owners, through the efforts of Friends.

In more recent times Friends in South Africa, with support from Quaker Peace & Service, have worked for reconciliation between races, and have assisted in relief work in townships such as Soweto and Crossroads. Quaker House, Cape Town, which appears in the panel, organises many activities directed towards peace.

Panel F19

Tasmania

James Backhouse (1794-1869), a York nurseryman, early felt a call to service in Australia. He had been only eighteen when, in response to the ministry of Stephen Grellet, he first sensed that he would have a call to a far-off country: three years later he saw this as being Australia. He later met Elizabeth Fry and became interested in the reformation of convicts.   He chose George Washington Walker (1800-1859) of Newcastle upon Tyne as companion, sailing for Van Diemen's Land (now Tasmania)in September 1831. Their aims were both religious and practical: to preach the Gospel to scattered settlers, to investigate the penal system, to enquire into the treatment of Aborigines and to promote temperance. They visited, often on foot, most of the penal settlements in Van Diemen's Land, New South Wales and Norfolk Island, Daniel Wheeler (see Panel F4) sometimes accompanying them. They made detailed reports and recommendations for the local authorities and informed London Yearly Meeting. Always they suggested reformation and re-education rather than punishment, with Mission schools for the Aborigines funded by the Government.

In 1832 Backhouse and Walker helped to establish the first Meeting in Australia at Hobart, Tasmania, buying a Meeting House among the gum trees in 1837. With only two other Friends, one a young girl, the Meeting was formed from "the convicted, the disowned, and the convinced" who needed to be educated in Quaker principles. The isolation of settlers added to the difficulties, involving the two men in travelling great distances, often walking twenty to thirty miles daily. "Backhouse" said an early historian "lifted up his heart to God and took his pocket-compass". They kept valuable journals, illustrating them and detailing Australian flora and fauna. Backhouse, a gifted botanist, returned to England in 1841, whilst Walker later settled in Tasmania, opening the first Savings Bank and supporting the development of education.

Panel F20

Friends in
Canada

The Society of Friends in Canada, like the modern nation itself, owes its origin to Loyalists who migrated to "Upper Canada" after the American War of Independence. Land was made over to them in 1800, partly used for Yonge Street Meeting House, Ontario, still in use today.

The centre of the panel portrays Camp Neekaunis, near Georgian Bay, a camp in the care of Canadian Yearly Meeting for educational and recreational programmes: the name is in the Huron language.

The Doukhobors were a Russian Christian group, whose pacifist philosophy and communal life made them anathema to the authorities. A number of concerned Friends responded to their plight, and in 1898 they were allowed to leave for religious freedom in Canada, taken there by British and American Friends. Their first school was in Nellie Baker's tent, as shown on the left of the panel; she and her cousin lived in another and held a dispensary in a third. Still a concern of Canadian Friends, the Doukhobor history has not been smooth.

Alma Dale (1855?-1930) travelled through the remote West, drawn long distances by her cream horses, to support and encourage scattered Friends. The Committee for Native Concerns works for reconciliation in issues, notably land rights, adversely affecting native people. The Micmac nation, with the salmon symbol, has in recent years been in dispute with the Quebec government over fishing rights. The salmon in the panel is drawn in the style of the Haida, natives of the north-west of British Columbia, whose decorative art is resurgent.

This panel was embroidered by Friends of fifteen meetings. The children's embroidery at bottom right represents fruit trees in Mexico. Victoria Monthly Meeting started a project to teach the Mexican school children gardening. Success led to hundreds of school orchards being cultivated.

FRIENDS in the NETHERLANDS

Jewish Children hidden in Quaker homes

The Pollatz family house Haarlem

1940-45

"God heeft mensen nodig."

Friends in the Netherlands

In 1655 one of the "First Publishers of Truth" was writing back to Swarthmoor Hall (see Panel C1) that "Many are raised up and moved for several parts: some are gone for France, and some for Holland". William Caton (1636-1665), a member of the Swarthmoor Hall household was, from the autumn of 1655, with other Friends active in travels and preaching in Vlissingen (Flushing), Middelburg, Rotterdam and Amsterdam, and before long a number of Quaker meetings were established. As the eighteenth century wore on, however, the number of Dutch Friends declined, their last epistle being received in London in 1788, their last member dying in 1850.

The rebirth of Quakerism in the Netherlands belongs to the 1920s. Very soon after its establishment in 1903, Woodbrooke College (see Panel B6) had so many Dutch students that when a separate men's hostel had to be built it was called Holland House. Some of these students, having become familiar with Quaker worship and practice, returned home and began to meet for worship with others who were likeminded. A yearly meeting was established in 1931, and in the 1930s Friends became increasingly involved in helping those refugees from Germany who had fled to the country. It was in part to further this work that a Quaker Centre (see Panel F16) was opened in Amsterdam in 1939. In May 1940 came the German invasion, bringing the refugees (some of whom already had their visas for the USA) into renewed danger. In May 1945, when the yearly meeting was again able to meet, it sent out an epistle including these words: "For five years we have been living under an oppression such as cannot be realised by those who have not experienced it, and now it has fallen from us suddenly. God gives us and the whole world again fresh chances".

In this panel we celebrate some of the chances which Netherlands Friends took in dark and difficult times, saving from Nazi persecution both adults and children by sheltering them in their own homes.

World Family of Friends

With Friends in some 56 countries, Quaker world membership is more than 216,000. They differ not only in language, culture and national allegiances, but also in the emphases they place on different aspects of Quakerism. Friends World Committee for Consultation (FWCC) was formed in 1937 to meet the need for communication; some 175 representatives appointed by Yearly Meetings and Groups affiliated with FWCC meet triennially in different parts of the world. The World Office is in London and each of the four autonomous Sections named in the panel has an executive office.

FWCC encourages inter-visitation and travel under religious concern; arranges conferences and gatherings; facilitates cooperation between mission and service bodies of Friends worldwide; produces publications in several languages; acts as Friends' official voice at the United Nations and its agencies; and forwards Friends' concerns such as peace and disarmament, abolition of torture, women's issues, racial equality and the right sharing of the world's resources.

Anne Wynn-Wilson designed this panel whilst attending the World Family Gathering at Waterford, Ireland, in 1986. She experienced the energy springing from the Seed, which inspired her to represent the Society as a great oak tree expressing the strength and diversity of its members, yet rooted in one source. The drawings of "Me and my friends" were collected, over two years, from Quaker children in the countries named, and the panel has been embroidered in Switzerland, Scotland, America and this country. The quotation from George Fox is a splendid note for the final panel, as appropriate today as it was three hundred years ago:

> Be patterns, be examples in all countries, places, islands, nations, wherever you come, that your carriage and life may preach among all sorts of people, and to them; then you will come to walk cheerfully over the world, answering that of God in everyone.

Final panel

Further Reading

The information that follows does not pretend to provide a complete list of works consulted in the research undertaken in the course of designing the panels. It aims to do no more than point to some books which will complement the panel by enlarging on the insights it seeks to convey or by recounting the story behind it. If the list seems formidable it is because it is assumed that some books will be available to some readers, others to others.

Essential to an appreciation of the Tapestry is John Ormerod Greenwood, *The Quaker tapestry* and the two volumes of London Yearly Meeting's book of Christian discipline, *Christian faith and practice* and *Church government*. References to these are given first, after the following abbreviations:

QT John Ormerod Greenwood, *The Quaker tapestry*, Impact Press, 1990
CFP London YM, *Christian faith and practice in the experience of the Society of Friends*, London YM, 1960
CG London YM, *Church government*, London YM, 1968; rev. ed., 1980

Following any references to these books are references to others frequently cited and therefore indicated by abbreviations:

BQ William Charles Braithwaite, *The beginnings of Quakerism*, Macmillan, 1912; 2nd ed., rev.
   by Henry J. Cadbury, Cambridge University Press, 1955; Sessions, 1981
BQS L.Violet Hodgkin, *A book of Quaker saints*, T. N. Foulis, 1917; repr. Friends Home
   Service Committee, 1972 (page ref. to 1917 ed. with the title of story to aid location in other editions)
CSQ Joseph Besse, *A collection of the sufferings of the people called Quakers*, 2 vol., Luke Hinde, 1753
GFQ Cecil W. Sharman, *George Fox & the Quakers*, Quaker Home Service, Friends United Press, 1991
JGF George Fox, *The journal of George Fox*, rev. ed. by John L. Nickalls, Cambridge
   University Press, 1952; repr. London YM, 1975
LPQ Rufus M. Jones, *The later periods of Quakerism*, 2 vol., Macmillan,1921
PP Edward H. Milligan, *The past is prologue: 100 years of Quaker overseas work, 1868-1968*,
   Friends Service Council, 1968
QP Stephen Allott, *Quaker pioneers*, Bannisdale Press, 1963
QPW Margaret E. Hirst, *The Quakers in peace and war*, Swarthmore Press, 1923; repr. Garland Publishing, 1972
QSI Arthur Raistrick, *Quakers in science and industry*, Bannisdale Press, 1950; repr.David & Charles, 1968
QSM A. Neave Brayshaw, *The Quakers: their story and message*, Allen & Unwin, 1921; page ref. to 3rd ed., rev.,
   1938; repr. Sessions, 1982
SPQ William Charles Braithwaite, *The second period of Quakerism*, Macmillan 1919, 2nd ed.,
   prepared by Henry J. Cadbury, Cambridge University Press, 1961; Sessions, 1979
SQ Elfrida Vipont, *The story of Quakerism*, Bannisdale Press, 1954; rev. ed., Friends United Press, 1977

These abbreviations are followed immediately by the page number (or, in the case of *CFP* and *CG*, the extract number).

Following these entries are references to other books: if portions only are relevant, the page numbers follow the date of publication, separated by a comma. In some few instances, deliberately rare and normally when there is no book dealing with the subject, reference is made to periodical articles.

At the end of these references notes will be found to help trace quotations on the panels. The first two or three words of the quotation are given, followed by the source: where it is in *CFP* or *CG*, reference is given to that, since each has a full list of sources and references. It should be noted that in a few cases the exigences of design have necessitated minor modifications in quotation: these, however, in no way affect the import or sense.

Prism "The Religious Society" *CFP*, preamble to ch. 1
A 1 *QT* 39-43; *CFP* 28-50; *BQS* 33-55 ("Pure foy, ma joye"); *QP* 9-18; *QSM* 33-5; *GFQ* 27-60; *JGF* 1-3; *SQ* 15-7
   T. Joseph Pickvance, *George Fox and the Purfeys: a study of the puritan background in Fenny Drayton in*
   the 16th and 17th centuries, Friends Historical Society, 1970
   Joan Allen, *Our George: the early years of George Fox the Quaker, 1624-45*, Bethany Enterprises,1990
   "There is one " *CFP* 5 "A church is", cf *JGF* 107
A 2 *QT* 44-6, 47-50, 51-8; *CFP* 22-5. *BQ* 60-2, 111-5, 241-78; *BQS* 301-20 (*'The saddest story of all'*); *QSM* 78,
   134-6; *SQ* 54-8, 75-7
   Mabel R.Brailsford, *A Quaker from Cromwell's army: James Nayler*, Swarthmore Press, 1927
   Geoffrey F. Nuttall, *James Nayler, a fresh approach*, Friends Historical Society, 1954

William G. Bittle, *James Nayler 1618-1660: the Quaker indicted by Parliament*, Sessions, Friends United Press, 1986
"There is a" *CFP* 25

A3   JAMES PARNELL: *QT* 62-4. *BQ* 188-93; *BQS* 255-83 ("Little James and his journeys","The first Quaker martyr"); *CSQ* i 190-2; *QSM* 81-2, 158, 174; *SQ* 43, 47-8
MEETING FOR SUFFERINGS: *QT* 74-6; *CG* 811. *SPQ* 615-6
N.C. Hunt, *Two early political associations*, Clarendon Press, 1961
"I must see" *BQS* 269;

A4   *QT* 184-7. *BQS* 403-25 ("Richard Sellar and the merciful man"); *CSQ* ii 112-20; *QPW* 80-4; *SPQ* 615-6
"I was to die" *CSQ* ii 117

A5   *QT* 184-7. *BQ* 402-4; *BQS* 379-401 ("The marvellous voyage of the good ship Woodhouse"); *SQ* 64
James Bowden, *The history of the Society of Friends in America* vol. 1; Charles Gilpin, 1850, 63-7
London YM, *Christian life. faith and thought in the Society of Friends*, 1922, 28-30; 1942 ed., 18-21
"Cut through" Bowden 64

A6   *QT* 107-16; *CFP* 46-51, 293, 315, 324, 410, 418, 441, 478, 532, 557 609. *LPQ* 23-5, 67-8, 315-7; *QP* 48-59; *QSM* 207; *SQ* 151-60
John Woolman, *The journal and major essays*, ed. Phillips P. Moulton, Oxford University Press, 1971; Friends United Press, 1989
Janet Whitney, *John Woolman, Quaker*, Harrap, 1943
Reginald Reynolds, *The wisdom of John Woolman with a selection of his writings as a guide to the seekers of today,* Allen & Unwin, 1948; repr. Quaker Home Service, 1988
Henry J. Cadbury, *John Woolman in England: a documentary supplement*, Friends Historical Society, 1971

A7   *QT* 200-3; *CFP* 625-8. *QPW* 507-15; *QSM* 328, 333-5; *SQ* 252-4, 256, 257-8
John William Graham, *Conscription and conscience: a history, 1916-1919,* Allen & Unwin, 1922
Denis Hayes, *Conscription conflict: the conflict of ideas in the struggle for and against military conscription in Britain between 1901 and 1939*, Sheppard Press,1949
Denis Hayes, *Challenge of conscience: the story of the conscientious objectors of 1939-1949*, Allen & Unwin, 1949
David Boulton, *Objection overruled*, Macgibbon & Kee, 1967
"Be faithful to" London YM epistle 1744

A8   *LPQ* 971-7; *QSM* 313-7; *SQ* 234-5
Society of Friends, *Report of the proceedings of the conference...held... in Manchester...1895,* Headley Brothers, 1895

A9   *CFP* 570-2; *CG* 943. *BQ* 478; *QSM* 128-30, 153-4; *SQ* 41, 135
Craig W. Horle, *The Quakers and the English legal system. 1660-1688,* University of Pennsylvania Press, 1988
G. B. Burnet, *The story of Quakerism in Scotland, 1650-1850*, Allenson, 1952
"We regard the" *CFP* 571

B1   *QT* 46-7. *BQ* 78-97; *BQS* 121-48 ("A wonderful fortnight"); *JGF* 106-10; *GFQ* 82-9; *SQ* 29-30
"Keep your feet" George Fox, *Epistles,* 1698, 152 (Ep. 195, 1660)

B2   MARY FISHER: *QT* 60, 63-4, 68-70. *BQ* 421-4; *BQS* 441-64 ("Silverslippers"); *QSM* 88; *SQ* 26, 41, 50-1, 61-2, 74
ELIZABETH HOOTON: *QT* 42-3,59-60,67-8. *SQ* 26
Emily Manners, *Elizabeth Hooton: first Quaker woman preacher,* 1600-1672; Friends Historical Society, 1914
MARY DYER: *QT* 66-7; *CFP* 33. *SQ* 64-5
ANN AUSTIN: *QT* 63-4. *BQ* 402; *QSM* 88; *SQ* 50-1

B3   *QT* 194-9; *CFP* 72, 576, 635. *LPQ* 629-47, 727-8; *QSM* 220, 285, 287; *SQ* 199
Keith Robbins, *John Bright*, Routledge, 1979
Nicholas Gillett, *John Bright, 1811-1889*, 1989; repr. from his *Men against war*, Gollancz, 1966, 41-55
"Alliances are" *Speeches*, ed. J. E. Thorold Rogers, 1868, i 468

B4   *QT* 76-9. *BQ* 569-70; *QSM* 73-82; *SPQ* 418-9; *SQ* 113-4
Luella M. Wright, *The literary life of the early Friends, 1650-1725,* Columbia University Press, 1932
Arnold Lloyd, *Quaker social history, 1669-1738*, Longmans, 1950, 147-56; ("The Quaker press")
"The principal" Robert Barclay, *Apology*, proposition 3, section 2

B5   *QT* 159-66; *CFP* 58-61. *BQS* 489-521 ("How a French noble became a Friend", "Preaching to nobody"); *LPQ* 206-8, 212-3, 342-5, 401-3, 875-7; *QSM* 228-9; *SQ* 176-80, 189, 194-5
William W. Comfort, *Stephen Grellet*, Macmillan, 1942
Stephen Grellet, *Memoirs of the life and gospel labours,* ed. Benjamin Seebohm, 2 vol., A. W. Bennett, 1860
"Proclaim unto" *CFP* 58

B6   *QSM* 319; *SQ* 236-7
Arnold S. Rowntree, *Woodbrooke: its history and aims*, Woodbrooke Extension Committee, 1923
Robert Davis (ed.), *Woodbrooke. 1903-1953: a brief history of a Quaker experiment in religious education,* Bannisdale Press, 1953
F. Ralph Barlow, *Woodbrooke, 1903-1978: a documentary account of Woodbrooke's third 25 years*, Sessions, 1982

B7   *QT* 238-9. *PP* 6-7, 10-22, 31-7, 45-57; *QP* 88-97; *QSM* 303-7, 341; *SQ* 211-6, 289
John Ormerod Greenwood, *Quaker encounters, vol. 2:Vines on the mountains: vol. 3: Whispers of truth,* Sessions, 1977-8
Charles Tyzack, *Friends to China: the Davidson brothers and the Friends' mission to China, 1886 to 1939,* Sessions, 1988
"Be patterns" *CFP* 376

B8   *QT* 207-8
      "World peace will" motto inscribed on Q-PAC van

C1 ⎫ *QT* 70-4; *CFP* 17-21, 401. BQ 98-110; *BQS* 149-83 ("Under the yew trees", "Bewitched", "The judge's return" ;
C2 ⎭   *QP* 19-29; *QSM* 72-4, 115, 135, 154-5; 180; *SQ* 31-9, 45, 79-80, 88-9, 90-2, 103-4, 111-2, 124, 134
      Isabel Ross, *Margaret Fell, mother of Quakerism,* Longmans, 1949; new ed., Sessions,1984
      Helen G. Crosfield, *Margaret Fox of Swarthmoor Hall*, Headley Brothers, 1913
      Ernest E. Taylor, *The valiant sixty*, Bannisdale Press, 1947; 3rd ed,rev,Sessions, 1988
      Elfrida Vipont, *George Fox and the valiant sixty,* Hamish Hamilton, 1975
      C 1 "You may meet" Ross 15, from "The testimony of Margaret Fox" in George Fox, *Journal,* 1694, iv
      "A matter of" *JGF* 174; cf *Journal*, 1694, reading "sixty"
      C2 "We are a" Ross 128   "Although I am" *CFP* 21

C3   Horsleydown: *QT* 82-3. *QSM* 149-50 .
      George Whitehead, *The Christian progress of that ancient servant of Jesus Christ*, assigns of J. Sowle, 1725, 341
      Children: *QT* 83-4. *BQS* 285-99.("The children of Reading meeting"); *CSQ* i 13-27,65-7; *SQ* 94-5, 121-2

C4   *QT* 84-8. *QSM* 147
      Hubert Lidbetter, *The Friends meeting house: an historical survey*, Sessions, 1961; 2nd ed., 1979
      Kenneth H. Southall, *Our Quaker heritage: early meeting houses built prior to 1720 and in use today*,
      Home Service Committee, Sessions, [1974]
      "Come with heart" *CG* 702 (Advices: section II)

C5   *QT* 235-9
      "We met together" *CFP* 184

C6   *CFP* 388; *CG* 980

C7   *CFP* 437-52. *LPQ* 706-10; *QSM* 210-1; *SPQ* 525-32;   *SQ* 162-5, 225
      W. A. Campbell Stewart, *Quakers and education as seen in their schools in England,* Epworth Press, 1953
      "whatsoever things" *CFP* 438

C8   *QT* 88-92; *CFP* 481-510; *CG* 881-4. BQ 144-6; *SQ* 60, 144, 222
      Arnold Lloyd, *Quaker social history, 1669-1738*, Longmans, 1950, 48-65 ("Marriage")
      "Seek to know" *CG* 702 (Advices: section I)   "Friends I take" *CG* 906 "We sensibly felt" *CFP* 488

C9   Elfrida Vipont Foulds, *The birthplace of Quakerism: a handbook for the 1652 country,* Friends Home Service
      Committee, 1952; 3rd ed., rev., Quaker Home Service, 1987
      "The Kingdom of"   *CFP* 184

C10   *QSM* 226-7, 318; *SQ* 240
      Friends Education Council, *Growing up in Quaker worship*, FEC, 1952
      "Watch with" *CG* 702 (Advices: section III)

C11   *QT* 79

D1   *QT* 43-4. BQ 56-7; *GFQ* 75-6; *JGF* 71-2; *SQ* 24
      "Be still and" *CFP* 303   "I saw an" *CFP* 7

D2   *QT* 224-7; *CFP* 433-4, 401. *QSM* 122-8, 190-5
      Verily Anderson, *Friends and relations: three centuries of Quaker families*, Hodder & Stoughton, 1980, 144-7
      Hubert F. Barclay and Alice Wilson-Fox, *A history of the Barclay family*, part 3, St Catherine's Press, 1934, 235-40
      "that the simplicity" *CFP* 433

D3   *QT* 60-2. BQ 158-9, 297-9; *CSQ* i 526-76; *SQ* 44, 71
      Stephen Allott, *Friends in Oxford: the history of a Quaker meeting*, (printed Gants Hill Press), 1952
      "Love, wisdom and" cf George Fox, *Epistles*, 1698, 308 (Ep. 276, 1669)

D4   *QT* 124-7. *QSI* 124-46; *SQ* 146
      Arthur Raistrick, *Dynasty of iron founders: the Darbys and Coalbrookdale,*
      Longmans, 1953; 2nd ed., rev., Sessions, 1989

D5   *QT* 128-31. *QSI* 35-242
      Isabel Grubb, *Quakerism and industry before 1800,* Williams & Norgate, 1930

D6   *QT* 127-8. *QSI* 70-82; *QSM* 137-9, 354
      Herbert Heaton, *Yorkshire cloth traders in the United States; 1770-1840* (Thoresby Society, 37), 1941
      "Not slothful" Romans 12: 7

D7   *QT* 131-4
      Paul H. Emden, *Quakers in commerce*, Sampson Low, 1939, 61-8
      Edward H. Milligan, *Quakers and railways,* Sessions, 1992
      Michael Farr, *Thomas Edmondson and his tickets,* The Author, 1991
      Geoffrey Hill, *The Worsdells: a Quaker engineering dynasty,* Transport Publishing Co, 1991
      "True godliness" *CFP* 395   "in their handiwork" Ecclesiasticus 38: 34

D8   *QT* 143-6. *QSI* 243-75; *SQ* 148-9
      E. Jean Whittaker, *Thomas Lawson, 1630-1691: north country botanist; Quaker and schoolmaster*, Sessions 1986 .
      R. Hingston Fox, *Dr John Fothergill and his friends*, Macmillan, 1919
      "the universe is" *QT* 146, from *Annual monitor* 1918, 10-1

D9   *QT* 146-8,151-5; *CFP* 470-7. *QP* 60-7; *QSI* 288-315; *QSM* 210, 212-3, 218n; *SQ* 147-9, 163-4, 246-7

Robert A. Clark and J. Russell Elkinton, *The Quaker heritage in medicine*, Boxwood Press, 1978

Amalie M. and Edward H. Kass, *Perfecting the world: the life and times of Thomas Hodgkin, 1798-1866*, Harvard University Press, 1988

Richard B. Fisher, *Joseph Lister. 1827-1912*, Macdonald & Janes, 1977

Fenner Brockway, *Bermondsey story: the life of Alfred Salter*, Allen & Unwin, 1949

Mary R. Glover, *The Retreat; York: an early Quaker experiment in the treatment of mental illness*, Sessions, 1984

Harold C. Hunt, *A retired habitation: a history of The Retreat. York*, H. K. Lewis, 1932

"True health springs" cf *CFP* 477

D10   *QT* 155-8; *CFP* 124, 138-47. *QSI* 270-5; *QSM* 217-8; *SQ* 174

A. Ruth Fry, *Quaker ways*, Cassell, 1933, 200-15 ("Quaker scientists")

"The immensities of" cf *CFP* 146

D11   *QT* 134-6. *QP* 98-106; *SQ* 146, 218-20

Arthur Raistrick, *Two centuries of industrial welfare: the London (Quaker) Lead Company, 1692-1905*, Friends Historical Society, 1938; 2nd ed., Moorland Publishing, 1977

Anne Vernon, *A Quaker business man: the life of Joseph Rowntree, 1836-1925*, Allen &Unwin, 1958; Sessions, 1982

Lewis E. Waddilove, *One man's vision: the story of the Joseph Rowntree Village Trust*, Allen & Unwin, 1954

A. G. Gardiner, *Life of George Cadbury*, Cassell, 1923

T. A. B. Corley, *Quaker enterprise in biscuits: Huntley & Palmers of Reading.1822-1972*, Hutchinson, 1972

D12   "The care of our planet" by Michael Thompson, in *Friends quarterly* xxvi 1-6 (January 1990)

"Befriending the earth: a theological challenge" by Rex Ambler, in *Friends quarterly* xxvi 7-17 (January 1990)

"Cherish the" *CG* 702 (Advices: Section IV) "Are you concerned" *CG* 703 (Query 19)

D13   Scott Bader Company, *A kind of alchemy: Scott Bader*, SBC, 1973

E1   *QT* 50-1; *CFP* 470. *BQS* 185-96 ("Strike again"); *GFQ* 103-4; *JGF* 125-9; *QSM* 37, 72

E2   *QT* 99-102; *CFP* 243. *QP* 41-7; *QSI* 82-7; *QSM* 203-4; *SPQ* 571-94; *SQ* 115, 132-4

George Clarke (ed.), *John Bellers. his life. times and writings*, Routledge, 1987

A. Ruth Fry (ed), *John Bellers 1654-1725, Quaker economist and social reformer: his writings reprinted, with a memoir*, Cassell, 1935

E3   *QT* 138-40. *QSI* 319-33; *QSM* 204; *SQ* 146

P. W. Matthews and Anthony W. Tuke, *History of Barclays Bank*, Blades, East & Blades, 1926

Humphrey Lloyd, *The Quaker Lloyds in the industrial revolution*, Hutchinson, 1975,157-275 ("This trade of bankering")

E4   *CFP* 573-7

Janet Arthur and others, *Six Quakers look at crime and punishment*, Quaker Social Responsibility & Education, 1979

E5 ⎫ *QT* 166-79; *CFP* 65-9,462. *LPQ* 350-67; *QP* 68-78; *QSM* 190-1; *SQ* 171-2, 178, 185-93
E6 ⎭

Janet Whitney, *Elizabeth Fry, Quaker heroine*, Harrap, 1937

June Rose, *Elizabeth Fry: a biography*, Macmillan, 1980

Elizabeth Fry, *Memoir of the life, with extracts from her journal and letters*, ed. by two of her daughters, 2 vol., Charles Gilpin, Hatchard & Son; 1847; 2nd ed., rev. and enlarged, 2 vol., 1848

E5 "Lord I believe" Mark 9: 24

E7   *QT* 227-30; *CFP* 453-7. *LPQ* 678-9,955-8; *QSM* 279, 308-10; *SQ* 218-22, 234, 245-6

J. F. C. Harrison, *Learning and living, 1790-1960: a study in the history of the English adult education movement*, Routledge, 1961.

G. Currie Martin, *The adult school movement. its origin and development*, National Adult School Union, 1924.

J. Wilhelm Rowntree and Henry Bryan Binns, *A history of the adult school movement*, Headley Brothers, 1903; repr. with a new introduction and additional notes by Christopher Charlton, University of Nottingham Department of Adult Education, 1985

E8   *QT* 211-5. *LPQ* 368-9; *QSM* 87; *SQ* 209

Isabel Grubb, *Quakers in Ireland; 1654-1900*, Swarthmore Press, 1927

Dublin YM, *Transactions of the Central Relief Committee of the Society of Friends during the famine in Ireland in 1846 and 1847*, Hodges & Smith, 1852

E9   *QT* 231-2; *CFP* 86; *CG* 788. *SQ* 248

Rosa Hobhouse, *Mary Hughes, her life for the dispossessed*, Rockliffe, 1949

Hugh S. Pyper, *Mary Hughes, a friend to all in need*, Quaker Home Service, 1985

E10   *QSM* 200ff 325; *SQ* 271-2

Joan Mary Fry, *Friends lend a hand in alleviating unemployment: the story of a social experiment extending over 20 years, 1926-1946*, Friends Book Centre, 1947

Barrie Naylor, *Quakers in the Rhondda, 1926-1986*, Maes-yr-haf Educational Trust, 1986

"The community is" *CFP* 545

E11   *QT* 140-2.   *LPQ* 796-7

David Tregonning and Hugh Cockerell, *Friends for life: the Friends Provident Life Office, 1832-1982*, Henry Melland, 1982

Elfrida Vipont Foulds and Edward H. Milligan, *So numerous a family: 200 years of Quaker education at Ackworth, 1779-1979*, Ackworth School, 1979, 24-5

"The true concern" *CFP* 363

E12   *QT* 148-51.   *LPQ* 335-47;   *QSM* 266n;   *SQ* 183-5, 194-6, 198

Helena Hall, *William Allen. 1770-1843*, Charles Clarke, 1953

L. Hugh Doncaster, *Friends of humanity; with special reference to the Quaker William Allen, 1770-1843*, Dr Williams's Trust, 1965

James Sherman, *Memoir of William Allen*, Charles Gilpin, 1851

William Allen, *Life, with selections from his correspondence*, 3 vol., Charles Gilpin, 1846-7

"cheerful, in the light" *CFP* 71

F1   *QT* 183-4; *CFP* 613. *BQ* 53-8; *BQS* 79-95 ("Taming the tiger"); *GFQ* 74-5; *JGF* 51-70; *QSM* 42-3; *SQ* 23-4

"Live in the" Advices, 1928, section II, cf *JGF* 65   "Deal Justly" *JGF* 37   "I spake to them" *JFG* 31

"Let your yea" James 5: 12, cf *JGF* 2, 38   "Justice Bennet" *JGF* 58

F2   *QT* 95-6. *CSQ* i 416-36; *QSM* 148; *SPQ* 69-74; *SQ* 105-6

Mabel R. Brailsford, *The making of William Penn*, Longmans, 1930, 312-22

F3   *QT* 103-7, 116-9. *QSM* 207-9; *LPQ* 320-37, 378-85, 594-5, 824-6

Thomas E. Drake, *Quakers and slavery in America*, Yale University Press, 1950

F4   *QT* 179-82; *CFP*-56. *LPQ* 877-85; *SQ* 195, 208-9

Daniel Wheeler, *Memoir of the life and gospel labours*, Harvey & Darton, Charles Gilpin, 1842

John Ormerod Greenwood, *Quaker encounters, vol. 2: Vines on the mountains*, Sessions, 1977, 117-52

Richenda Scott, *Quakers in Russia*, Michael Joseph, 1964

"God's love enableth" *CFP* 56

F5   *QT* 190-2. *LPQ* 725-6; *QPW* 256-9; *SQ* 205

Peter Brock, *The Quaker peace testimony, 1660 to 1914*, Sessions, 1990, 265-75 ("English Quakers in the Crimean War")

Griselda Fox Mason, *Sleigh ride to Russia: an account of the Quaker mission to St Petersburg*, Sessions, 1985

"O mighty prince" *QPW* 535 (text of address in full)

F6   *QT* 215-6; *CFP* 663. *SQ* 279, 287

Elfrida Vipont Foulds and others, *Mount Street. 1830-1930*, Mount Street Centenary Committee, 1930, 12

Lawrence Darton, *An account of the work of the Friends Committee for Refugees & Aliens, first known as the Germany Emergency Committee of the Society of Friends, 1933-1950*, FCRA, 1954

"Bertha L. Bracey, friend of the oppressed" by Alex Bryan, in *Friends quarterly*, xxvi 233-41 (January 1991)

"Yealand School closes" by E. V. F[oulds], in *Friend*; cii 537-8

"Our life is" *CFP* 404

F7   *QT* 216-9; *CFP* 663. *PP* 24-5, 28-30,40-4; *QPW* 497-501; *SQ* 257-61, 279-80, 282-6, 288

John Ormerod Greenwood, *Quaker encounters. vol. 1: Friends and relief*, Sessions, 1975

William K. Sessions, *They chose the star*, Friends Relief Service, 1944; 2nd ed., enlarged, Sessions, 1991

A. Ruth Fry, *A Quaker adventure: the story of nine years' relief and reconstruction*, Nisbet, 1926

Roger C. Wilson, *Quaker relief: an account of the relief work of the Society of Friends, 1940-1948*, Allen & Unwin, 1952

Margaret McNeill, *By the rivers of Babylon: a story of relief work among the displaced persons of Europe*, Bannisdale Press, 1950

Stanley Smith, *Spiceland Training Centre; 1940-1946: cups without saucers*, Sessions, 1990

F8   *QT* 219-22. *PP* 38; *QP* 107-15; *QPW* 501-3; *QSM* 328; *SQ* 256-7, 278-82

Meaburn Tatham and James E. Miles, *The Friends' Ambulance Unit; 1914 - 1919*, Swarthmore Press, (1919)

A. Tegla Davies, *Friends Ambulance Unit: the story of the FAU in the second world war, 1939-1946*, Allen & Unwin, 1947

F9   *QT* 222-3.

"Quaker Cottage 10 Years on" by Vincent Pent, in *Friend* cxlviii 1433-5 (9 November 1990)

F10   *QT* 119-20. *LPQ* 575-83; *QP* 79-87; *SQ* 203

Henrietta Buckmaster, *Out of the house of bondage: the story of the famous underground railroad of the American negro slaves*, Gollancz, 1943

William Still, *The underground rail road: a record of facts. authentio narratives, letters, &c.*, Porter & Coates, 1872

Levi Coffin, *Reminiscences of Levi Coffin. the reputed president of the underground railroad*, Sampson Low, 1876; repr Friends United Meeting, 1991

"Thou shalt not" Deuteronomy 23: 15

F11   *QT* 96-9; *CFP* 39, 588. *QP* 30-40; *QPW* 353-68; *QSM* 93-9; *SPQ* 402-15; *SQ* 116-21,135-6

Edwin B. Bronner, *William Penn's "Holy experiment the founding of Pennsylvania, 1681-1701*, Temple University Publications, 1962

Peter Brock, *The Quaker peace testimony, 1660-1914* Sessions, 1990, 87-101 ("The pacifist ethic and Quaker Pennsylvania: the first phase")

F12   *QT* 188-90. *LPQ* 759-62; *QPW* 466-8

Edouard A. Stackpole, *Whales and destiny*, University of Massachusetts Press, 1972

Flora Thomas, *The builders of Milford,* Pembrokeshir Telegraph, 1920; repr Western Telegraph, 1952

Stephen Griffith, *A history of Quakers in Pembrokeshire*, Milford Haven PM, 1990

"Bring the whole" *CG* 702 (Advices: section IV)

F13   *QT* 235

T. Mardy Rees, *A history of the Quakers in Wales and their emigration to North America,* Spurrell & Son, 1925

Evelyn S. Whiting, Ronald Morris and John R. Hughes, *The background of Quakers in Wales and the border,* Wales & Western Conference, 1952

"The Quakers of Merioneth during the 17th century" by J. Gwynn Williams, in Jnl Merioneth Historical & Record Soc. viii 122-56, 312-39 (1978, 1979)

F14   *QT* 237

Margaret West and Ruth M. Fawell, *The story of New Zealand Quakerism. 1842-1972*, New Zealand YM, 1973

F15   *QT* 203-6;   *CFP* 664-6.   *QP* 116-25

John S. Hoyland, *Digging with the unemployed,* Student Christian Movement Press;1 934

Reginald Reynolds, *John Somervell Hoylan*d, Friends Home Service Committee, 1958

F16   *QT* 208-10.   *SQ* 263-4

Willis H. Hall, *Quaker international work in Europe since 1914,* Reunies de Chambery, 1938

"Quaker peacemaking at the diplomatic level" by Peter Herby, in *Friends quarterly;* xxvi, 83-8 (April 1990)

"True peace cannot" *CFP* 621

F17   *QT* 206-7

"We utterly deny" *CFP* 614

F18   *SQ* 273-4, 295-6

Herbert M. Hadley, *Quakers world wide: a history of Friends World Committee for Consultation*, FWCC and Sessions, 1991

F19   *QT* 199-200

Hope Hay Hewison, *Hedge of wild almonds: the pro-Boers and the Quaker conscience. 1890-1910*, James Currey, 1989

F20   *QT* 237.   *SQ* 208

William N. Oats, *Backhouse and Walker: a Quaker view of the Australian colonies, 1832-1838,* Blubber Head Press, Australia YM, 1981

William N. Oats, *A question of survival: Quakers in Australia in the nineteenth century*, University of Queensland Press, 1985, 78-169

F21   *QT* 237-8

Arthur Garratt Dorland, *A history of the Society of Friends (Quakers) in Canada,* Macmillan Co. of Canada, 1927

Fred Haslam, *A record of experience with Canadian Friends (Quakers) and the Canadian ecumenical movement, 1921-1967,* Woodbrooke, 1970

F22   Christina Yates (ed.), *Friends in Europe,* Friends World Committee for Consultation, 1946, 35-8

World   *QT* 234-9; *CFP* 670-7

family   Herbert M. Hadley, *Quakers world wide: a history of Friends World Committee for Consultation,* FWCC and Sessions, 1991

Friends World Committee for Consultation, *Finding Friends around the world: handbook of the Religious Society of Friends (Quakers),* FWCC, 1988

"Walk cheerfully" *CFP* 376

INDEX

(Titles of panels are in italics)